Michael Steiner

SCULPTURE AND PAINTINGS

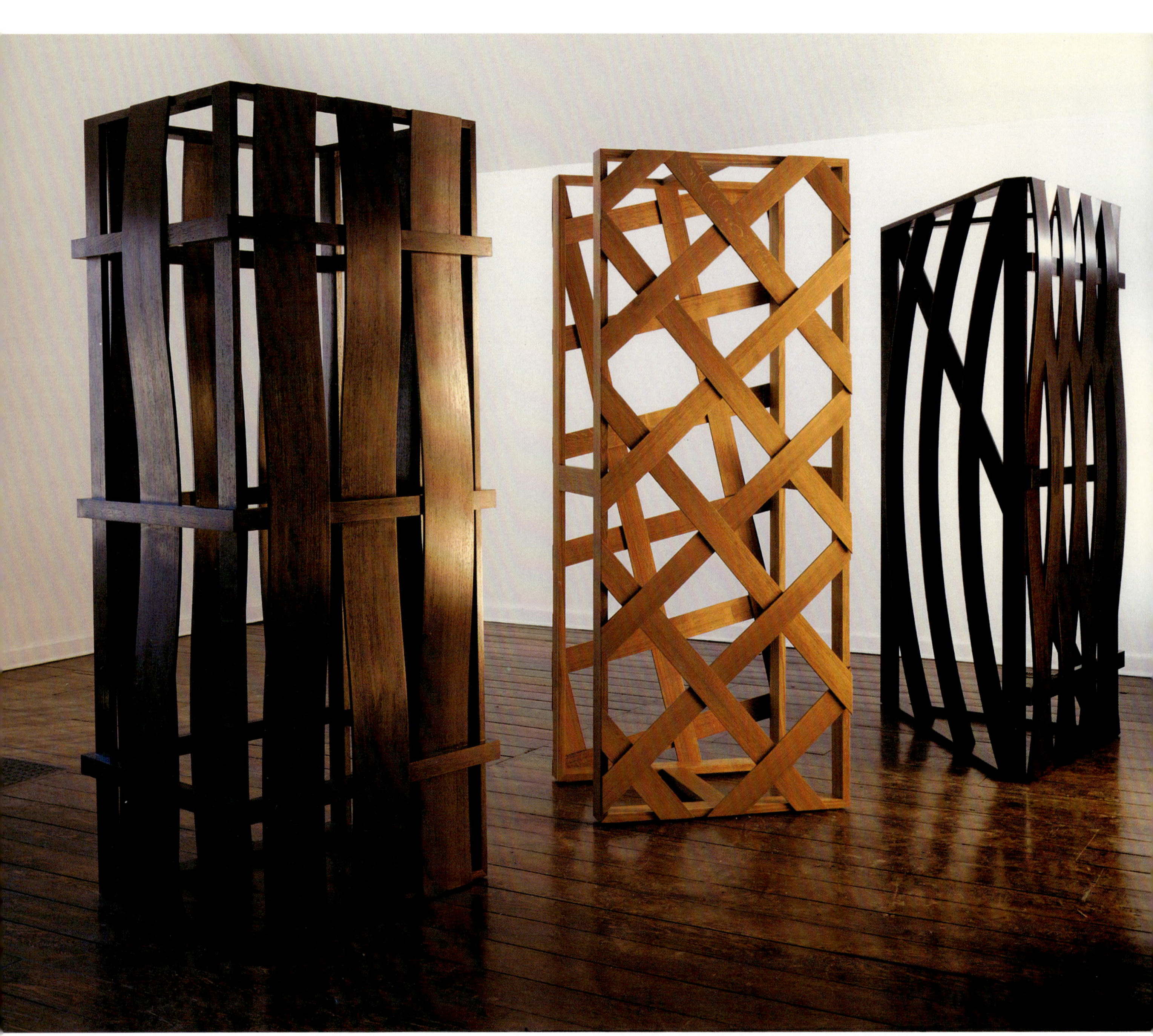

Michael Steiner

SCULPTURE AND PAINTINGS

SALANDER-O'REILLY

NEW YORK

This catalogue accompanies an exhibition from
March 28–April 29, 2006 at

SALANDER-O'REILLY GALLERIES, LLC
22 East 71 Street New York, NY 10021
Tel (212) 879-6606 Fax (212) 400-4490
WWW.SALANDER.COM
Gallery hours: Monday–Saturday 9:30 to 5:30

Michael Steiner: Sculpture

For the last ten-or-so years Michael Steiner has been involved with a new set of sculptural motifs characterized by his use of repetitive forms and cutouts as the compositional components of his sculptures. These highly optical, flat-patterned elements are employed here in a series of bronze pedestal sculptures, as well as a series of large freestanding works in wood. This catalogue presents the last four years of the artist's work. Steiner's series of lattice boxes, or, more properly, "cages," allude to the permutations of latticework in architecture, and evoke decorative patterns of ancient window frames or stained-glass leading. Steiner plays off the extreme flatness of layered pattern against our shifting visual experience as we move 360-degrees around the sculpture. In a sense, these works are a logical evolution from the early serial imagery of his minimalist sculptures from the sixties, and the tough, door-like forms of his late seventies "backs."

Steiner has always been a highly sophisticated thinker about art in general and sculpture in particular. He understands, as did Matisse before him, that a Western artist may potentially use the decorative to address primary issues of plastic expression, such as positive versus negative space, the horizontal and the diagonal, the curved against the straight, and how to construct a solid visual space out of transparency. With the line of his cages, Steiner has taken the sculpture imperative of drawing in space literally, and, in the process, condensed his sensibility into perhaps his most taut forms yet. Possibly the most elegant development in this series is Steiner's group of large-scale wood sculptures that actualize the furniture-like qualities of his recent bronzes. A master of bronze and welded steel, Steiner significantly lightens the density of his work in these highly refined wood pieces. In a 2005 review, a critic noted that Steiner's sculpture echoed "the shells of dilapidated, abandoned industrial buildings . . . ," referring perhaps unintentionally to the way effective art imposes an artist's perception on how we see the world. With Steiner's new work, he has achieved a kind of tension, humor, and rigor that both knocks us out and makes us chuckle in recognition. We see these sculptures by looking into them, and, with this porosity, Steiner shifts the way we experience sculpture and ultimately, the world.

Steven Harvey

1. *The Forest is Holy II*, 2005. Wood (wenge), 90 x 33 x 38½ inches

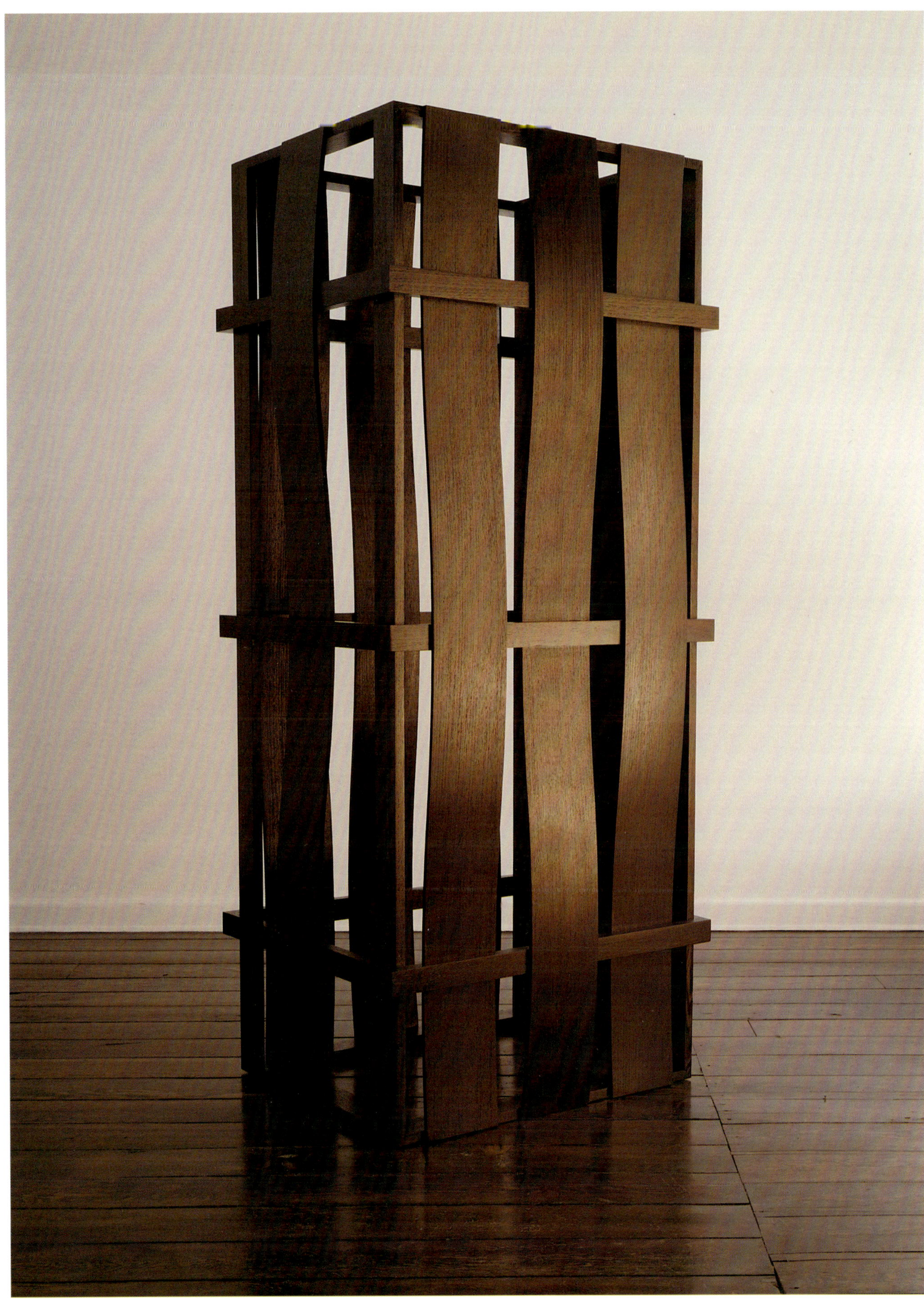

2. *Murmur in My Sleep II*, 2005. Wood (wenge), 84 x 28 x 36 inches

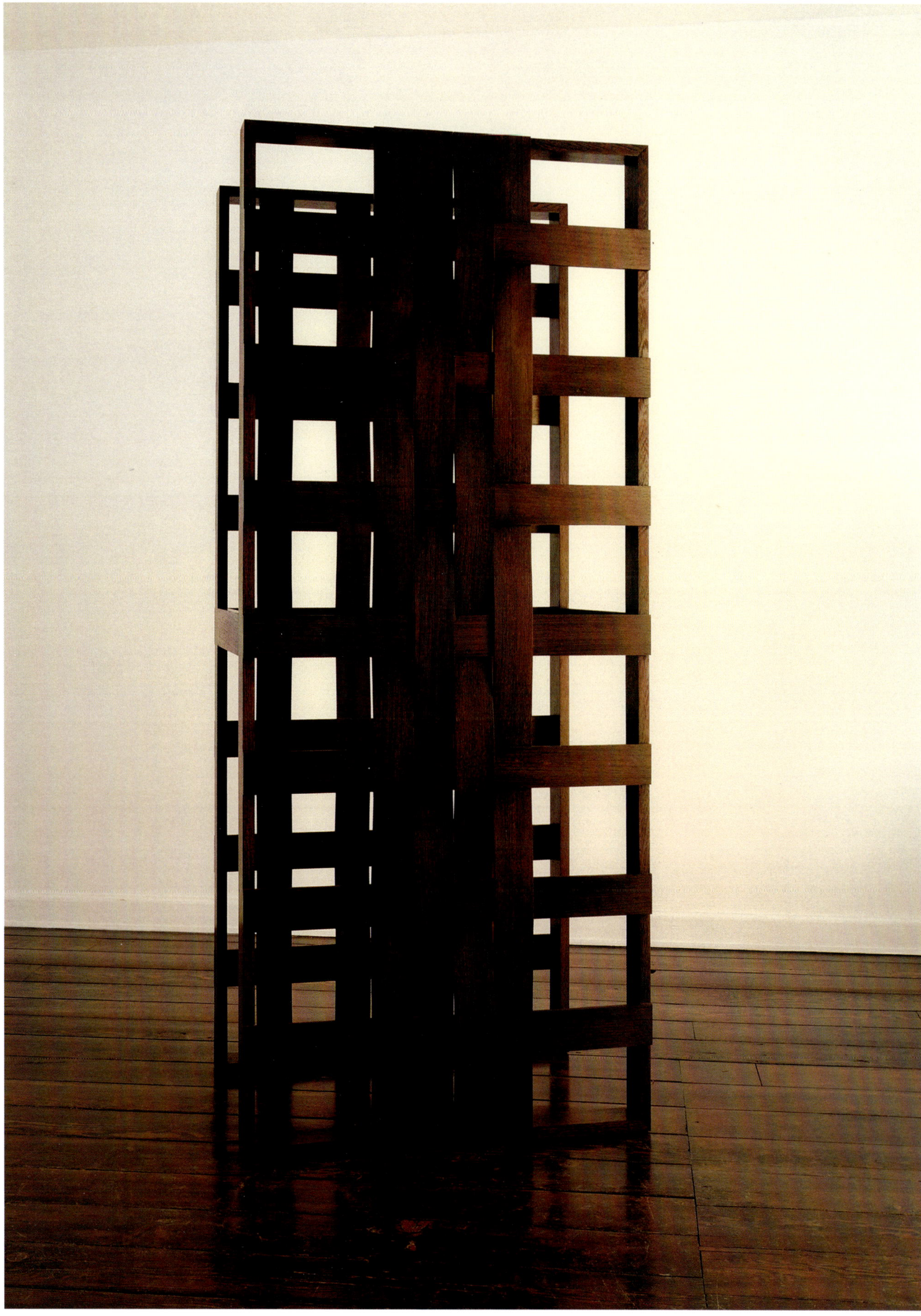

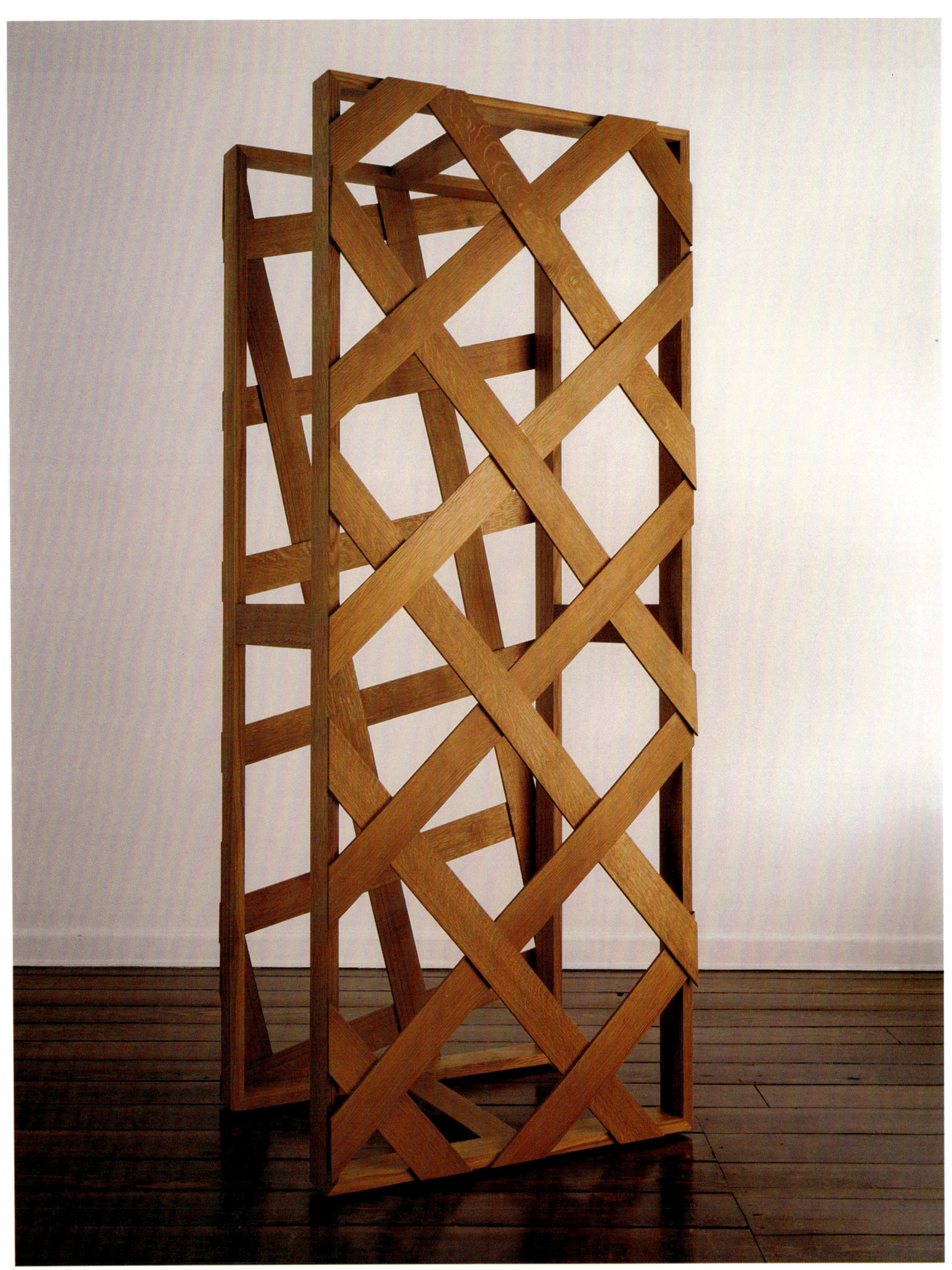

3. *Figure Turned Round II*, 2005. Wood (black oak), 90 x 28 x 37 inches

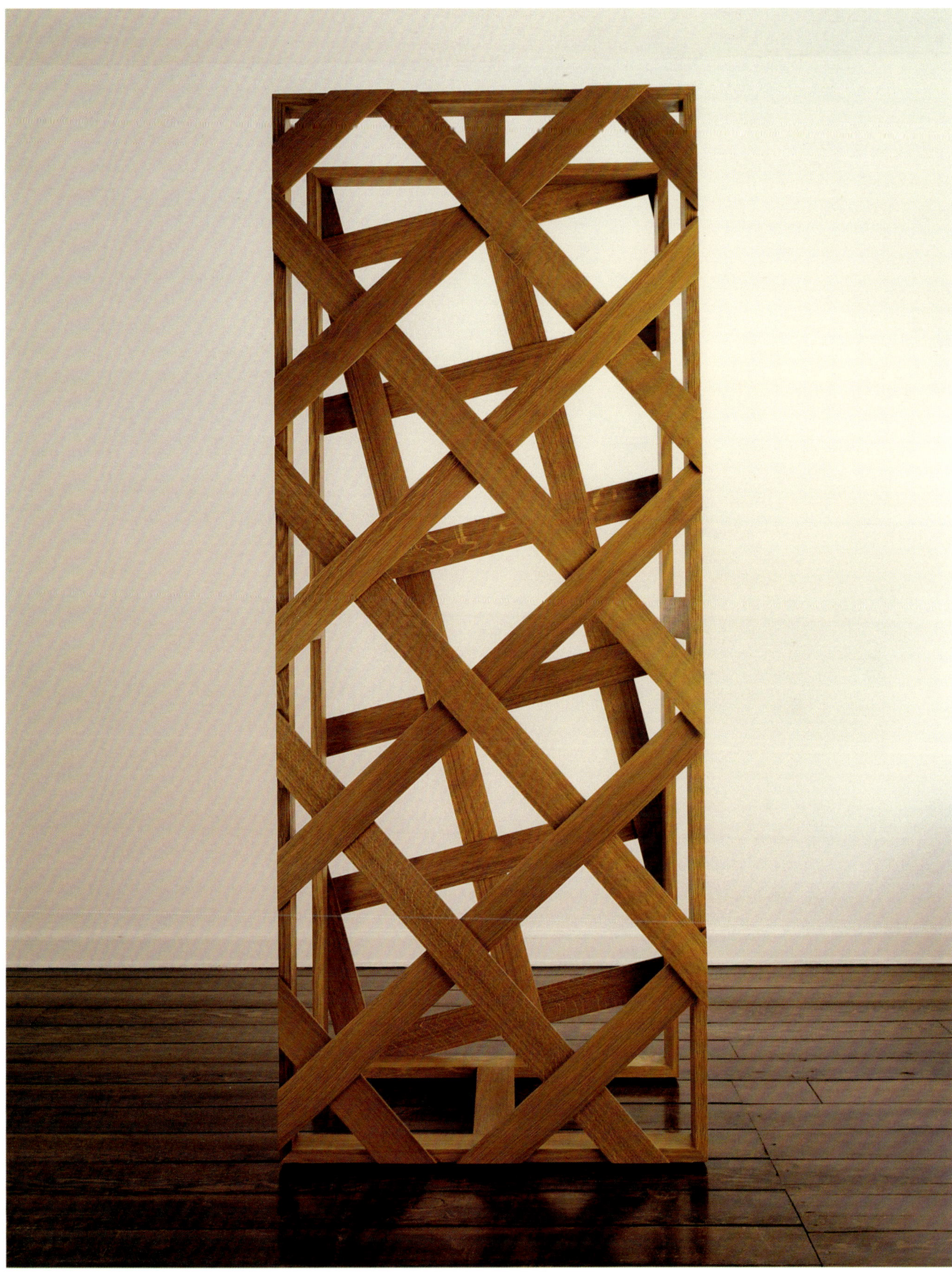

4. *Murmur in My Sleep III*, 2005. Wood (birch and plywood), 72¾ x 38 x 29½ inches

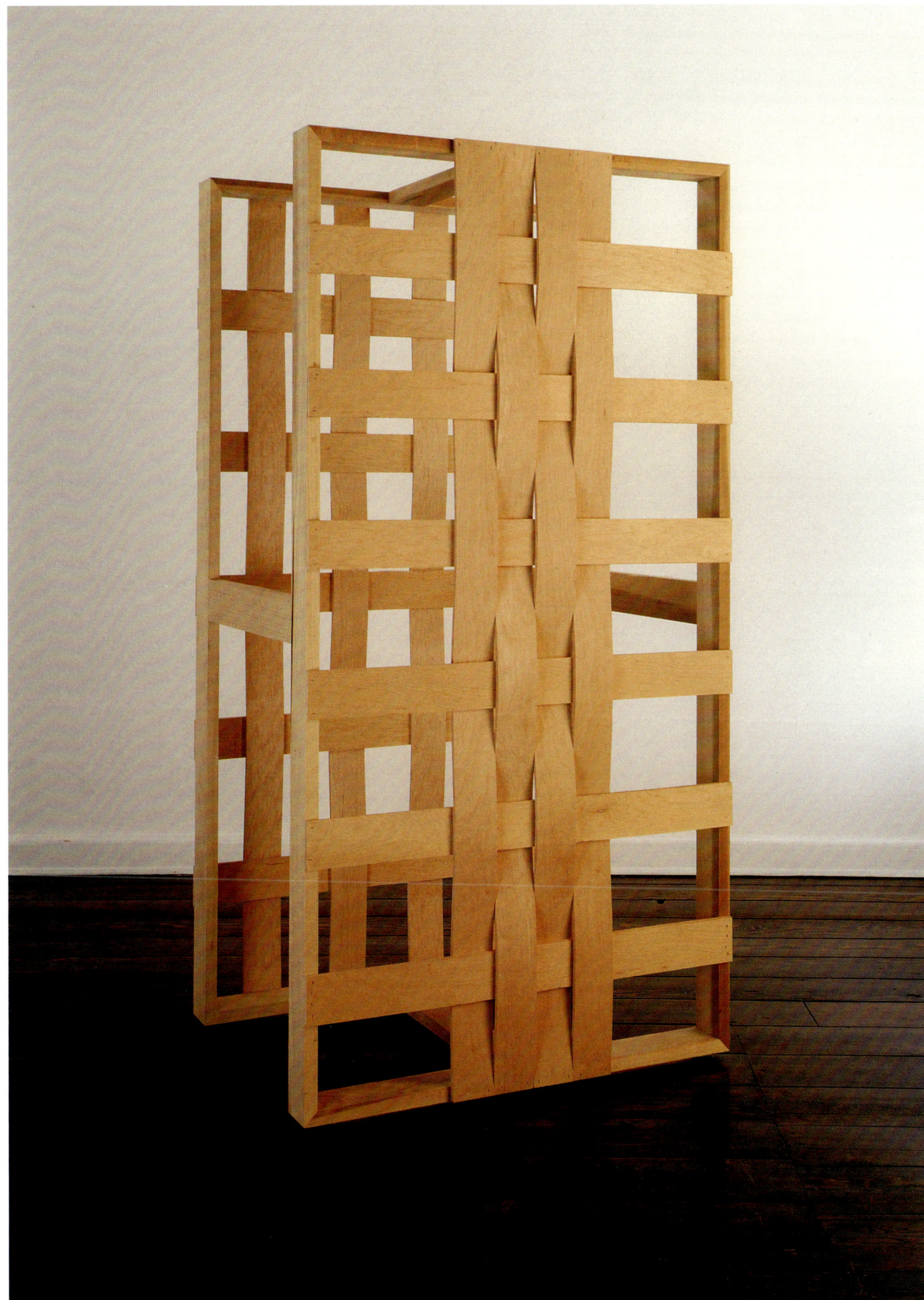

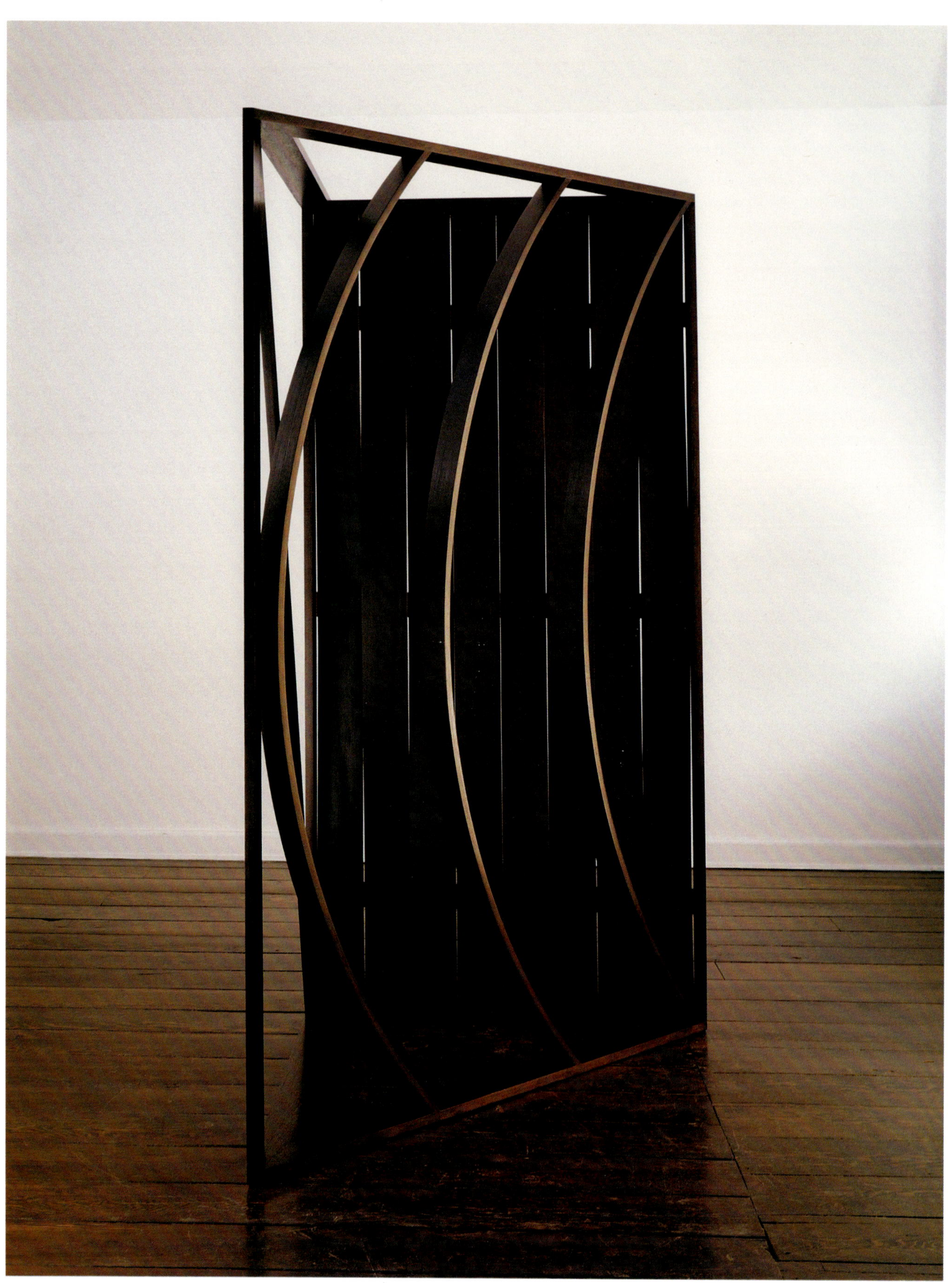

5. *Speed Forth II*, 2005. Wood (wenge), 90 x 45 x 46½ inches

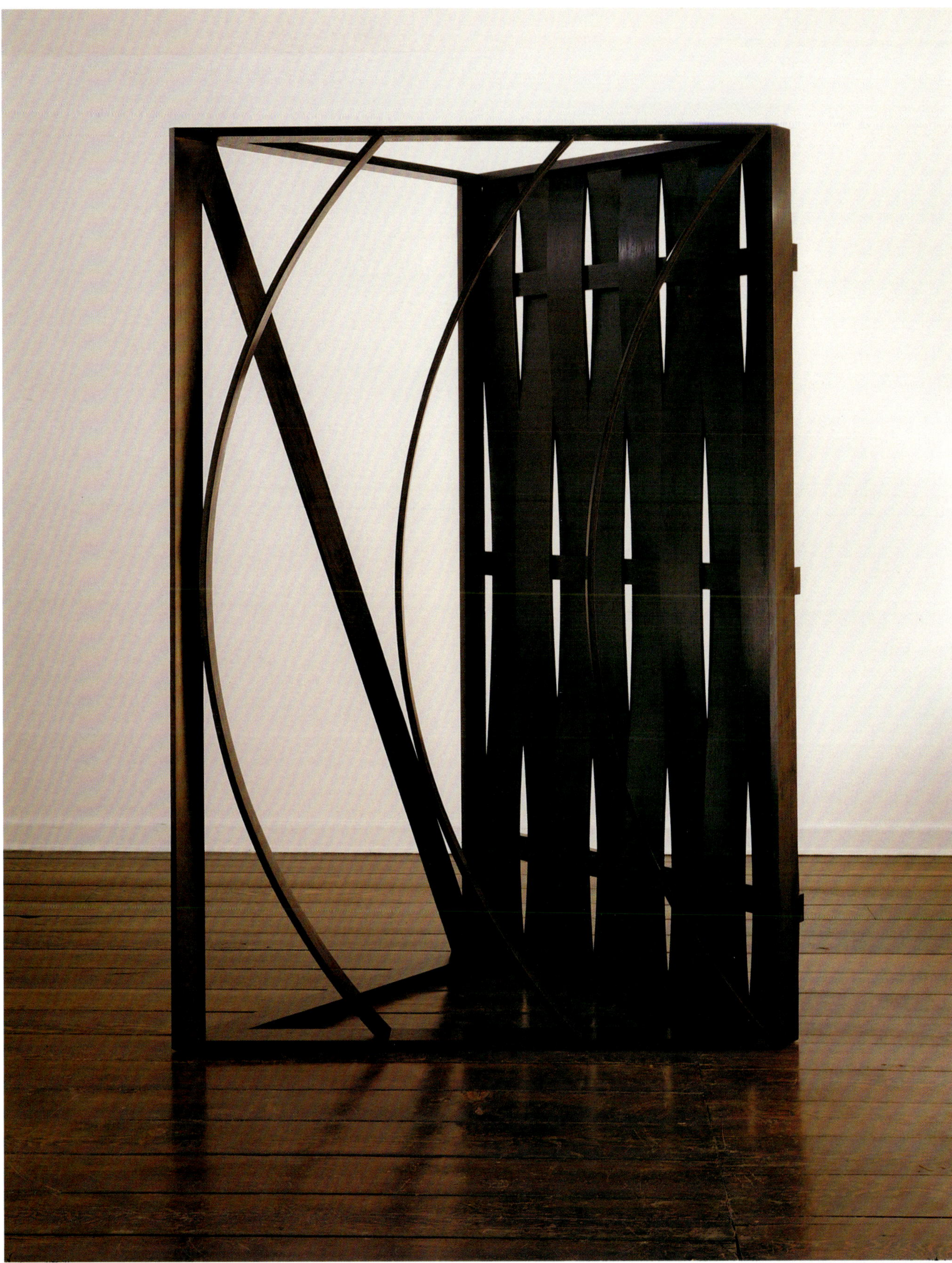

6. *The Forest is Holy*, 2005. Bronze, 33 x 15½ x 19¾ inches, edition of 6

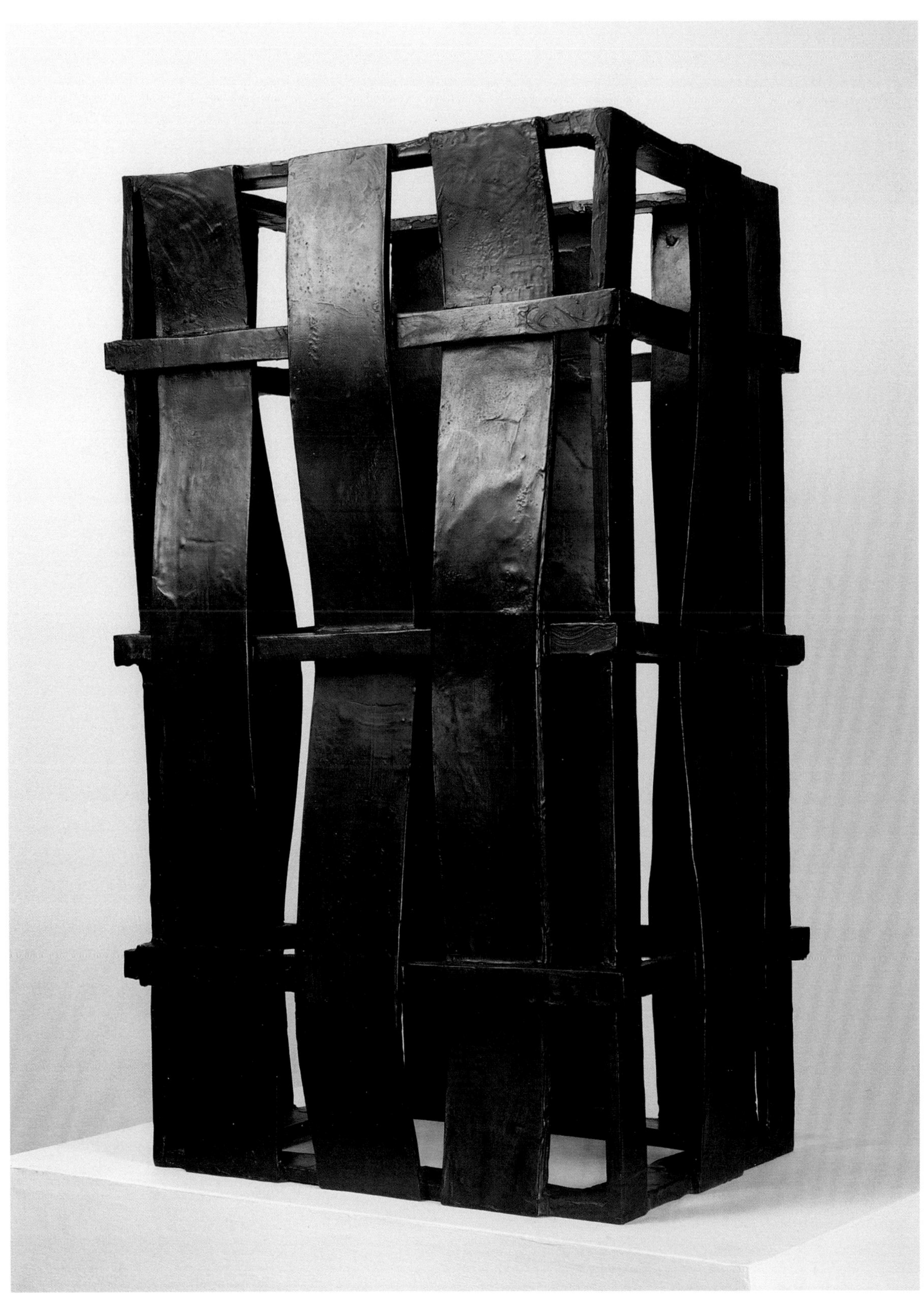

7. *Murmur in My Sleep*, 2005. Bronze, 29¾ x 15½ x 18¾ inches, edition of 6

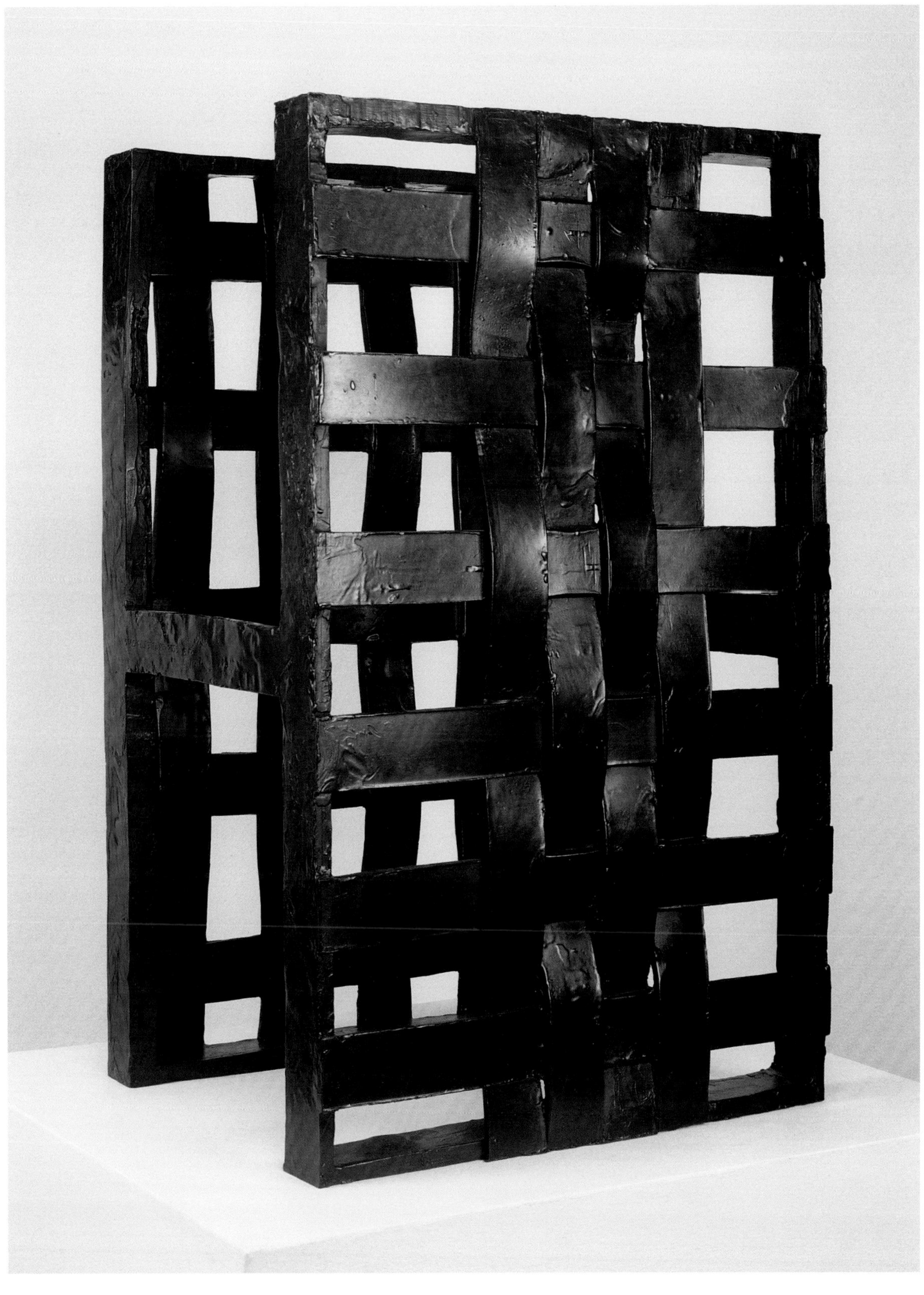

8. *Zero on the Bone*, 2005. Bronze, 33½ x 18 x 18½ inches, edition of 6

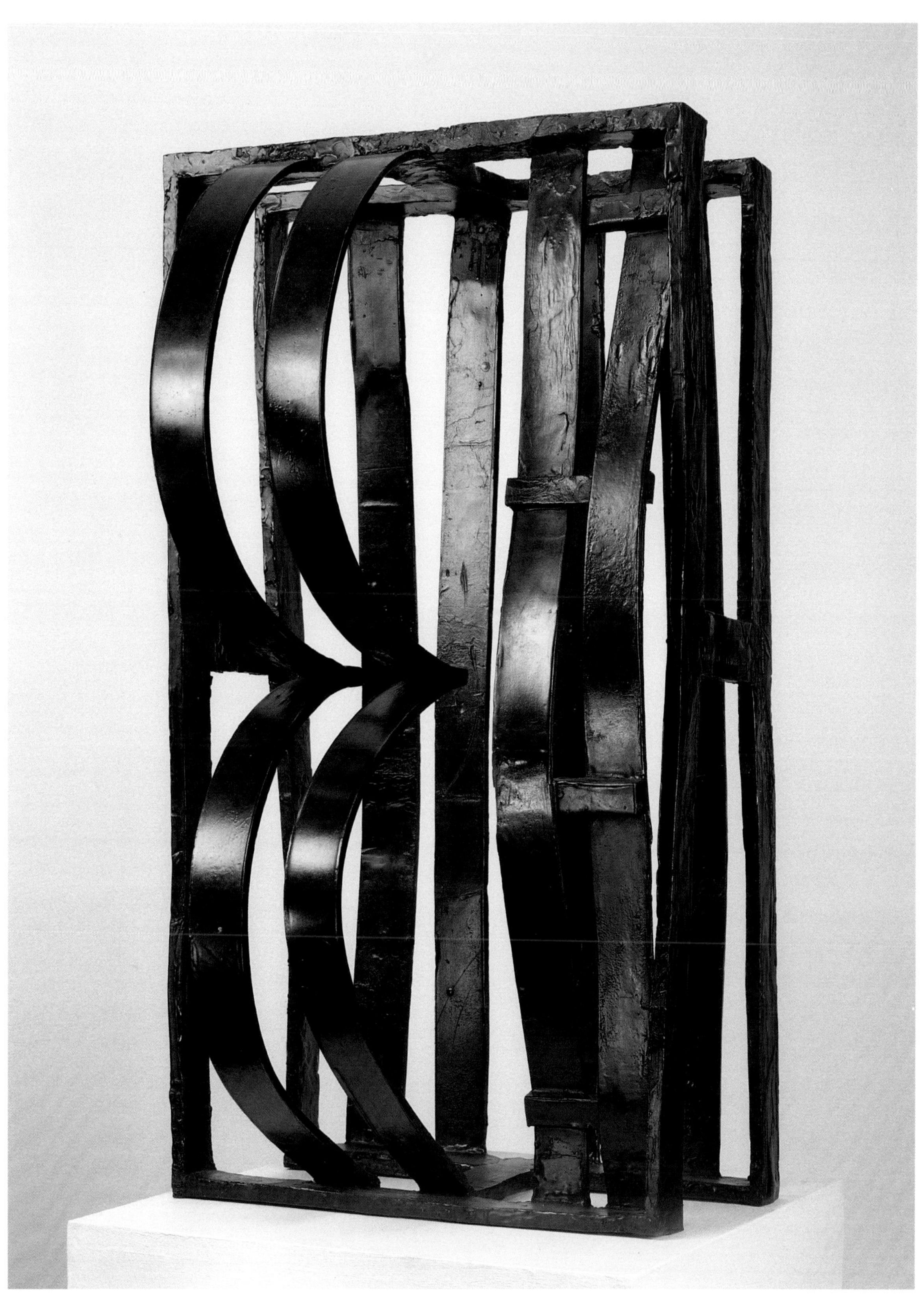

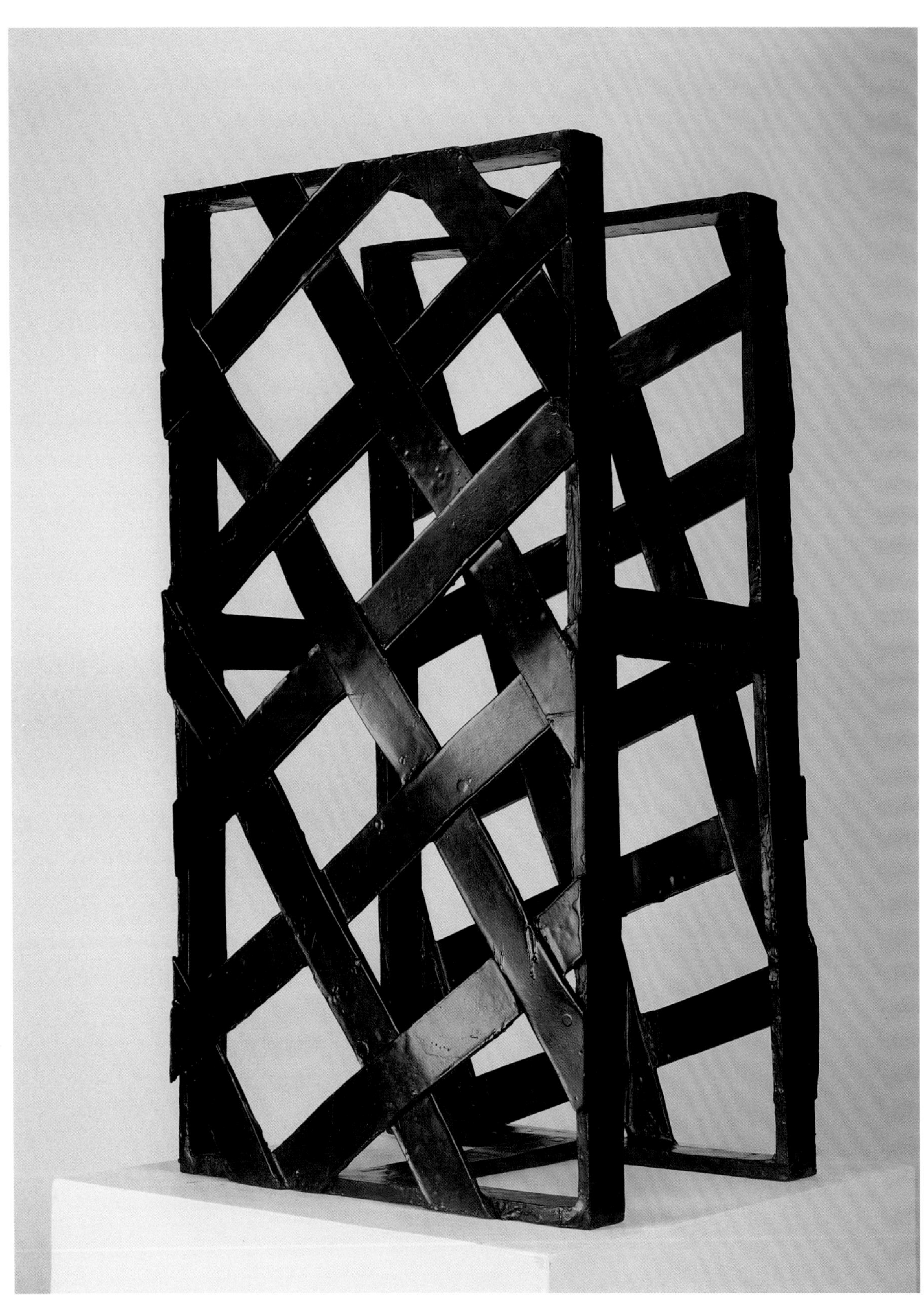

9. *Figure Turned Round*, 2005. Bronze, 33½ x 18½ x 14¾ inches, edition of 6

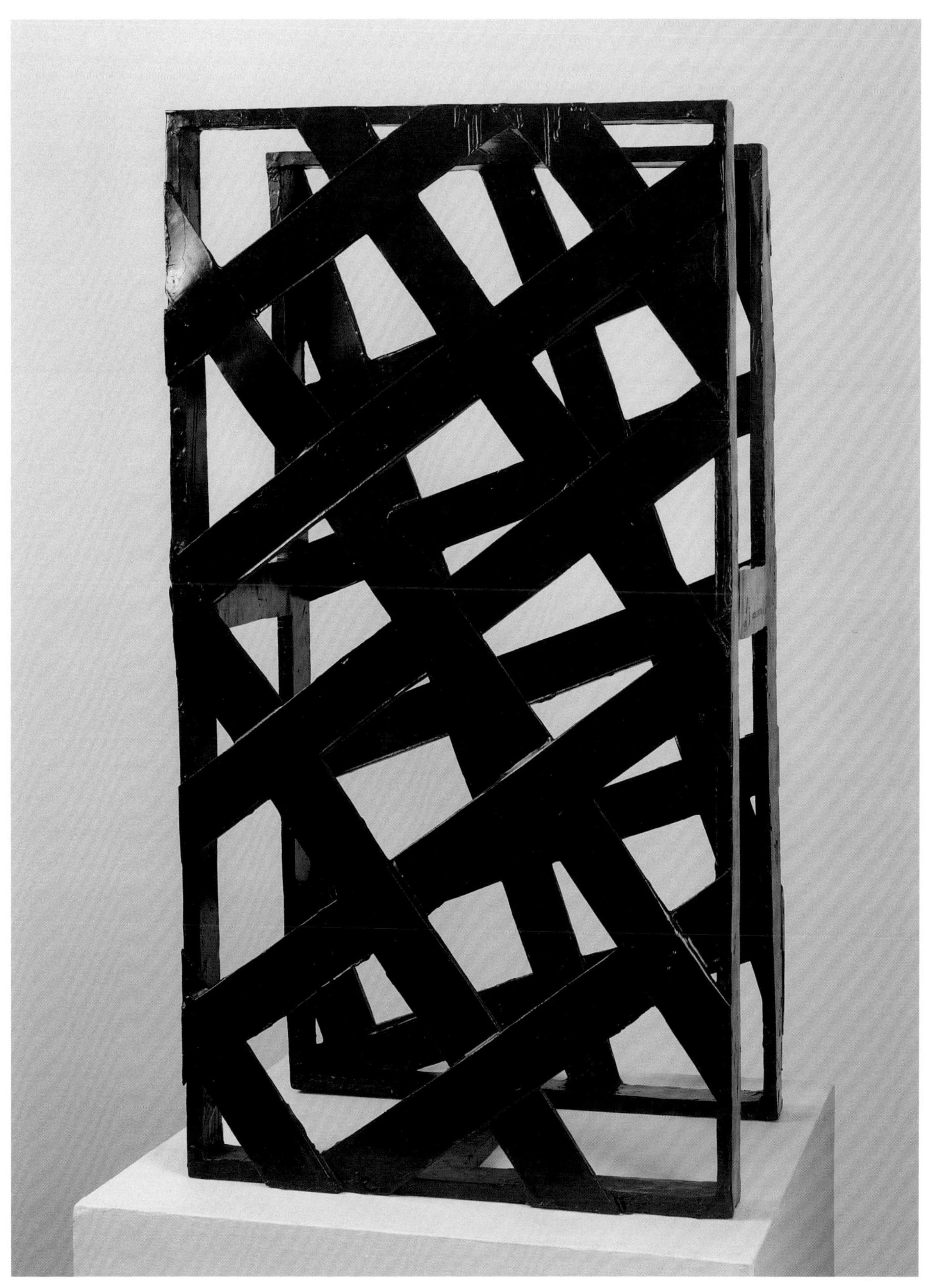

10. *Night to Overflow*, 2005. Bronze, 33½ x 9½ x 17¾ inches, edition of 6

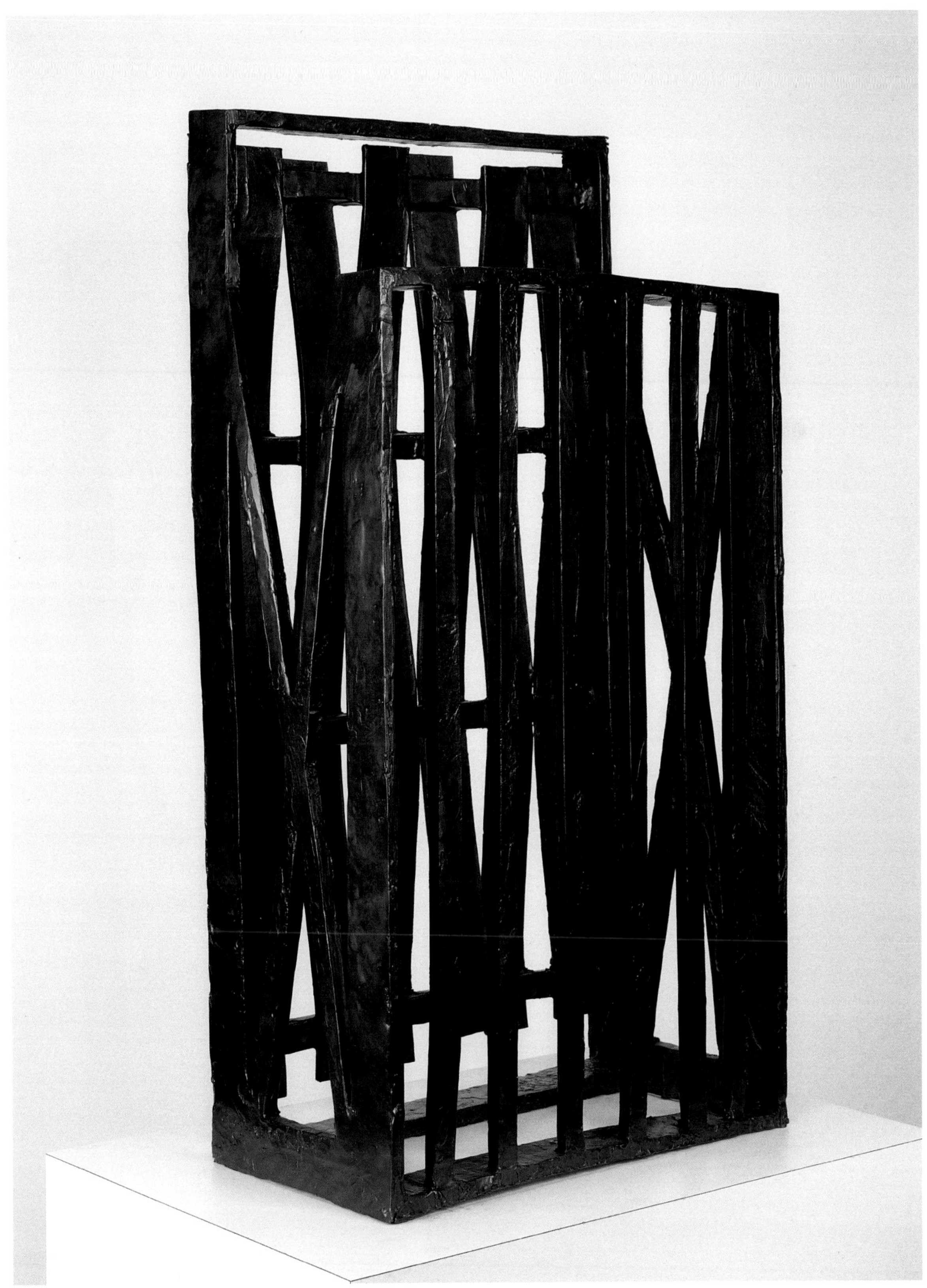

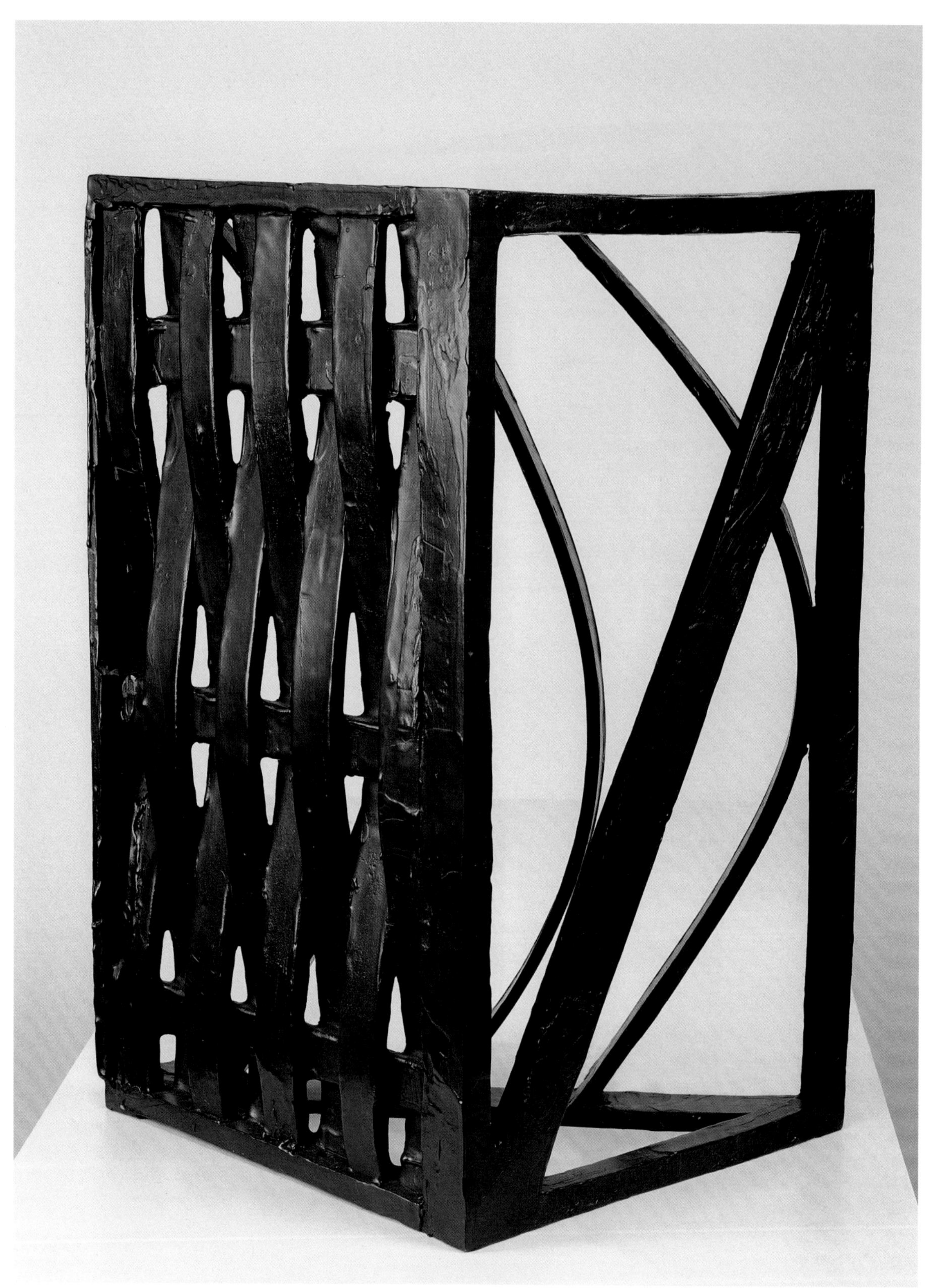

11. *Speed Forth I*, 2005. Bronze, 17¾ x 10 x 15 inches, edition of 6

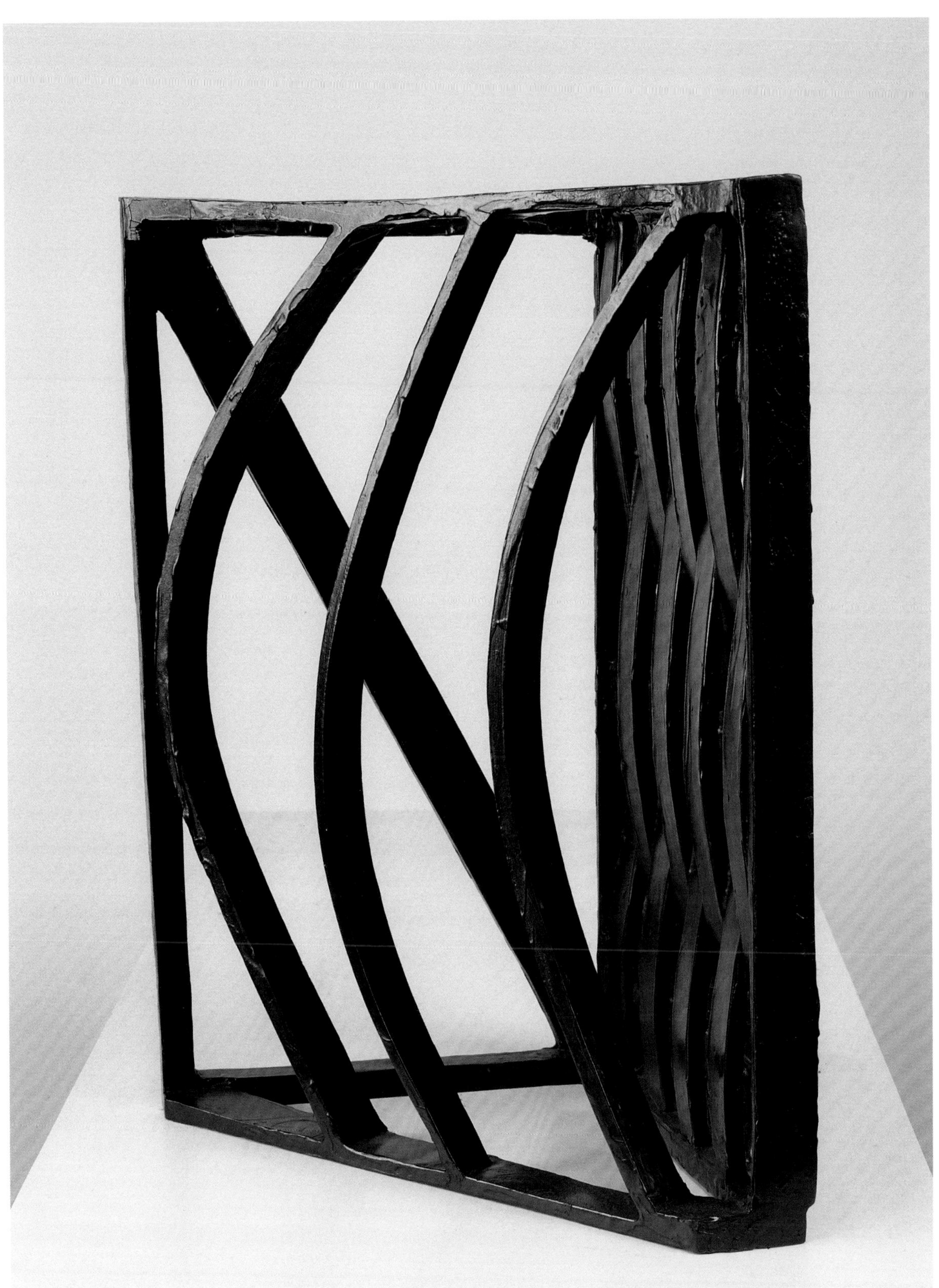

12. *Bones and Dust*, 2003. Bronze, 34 x 16¾ x 10¼ inches, edition of 6

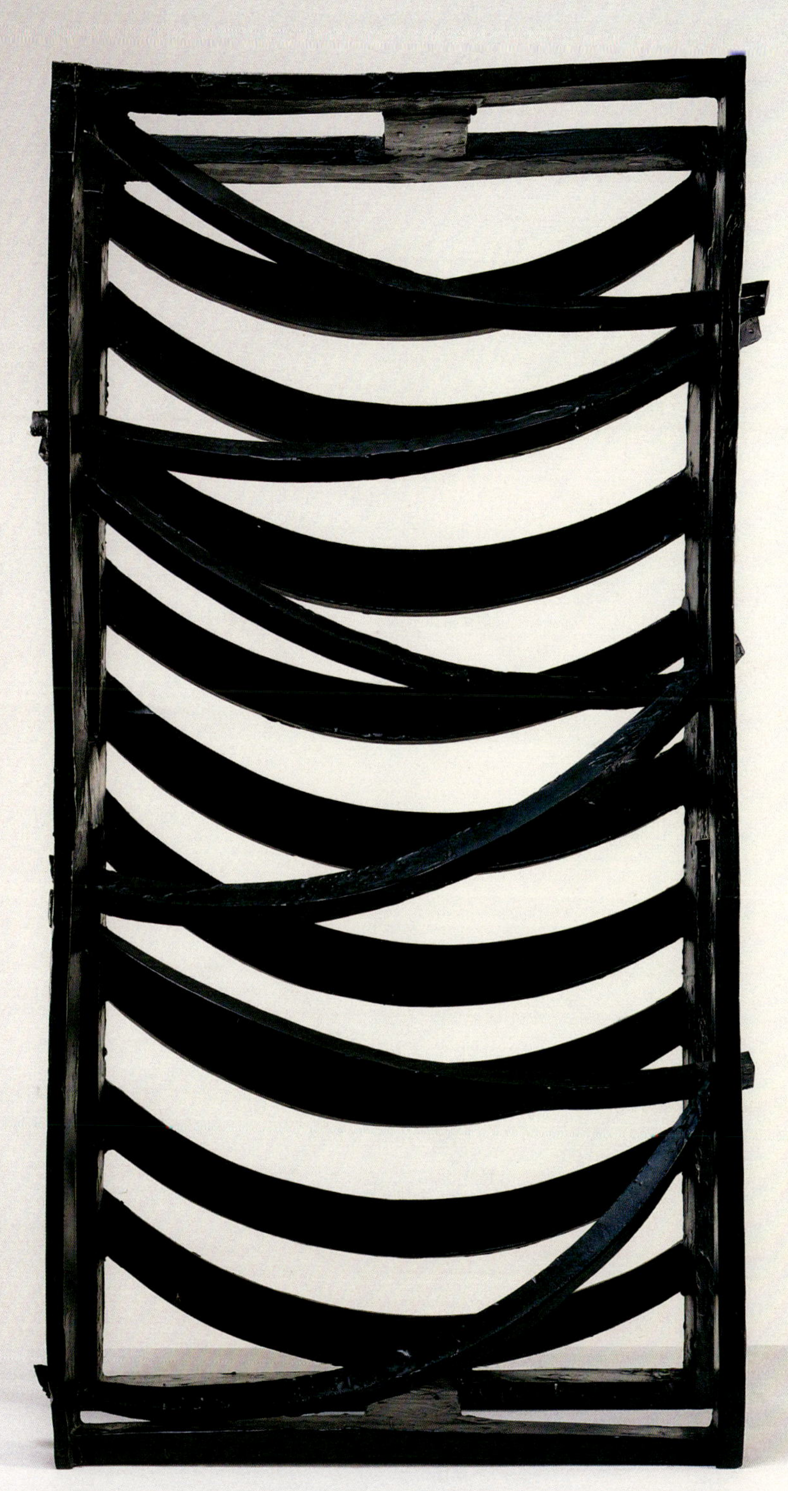

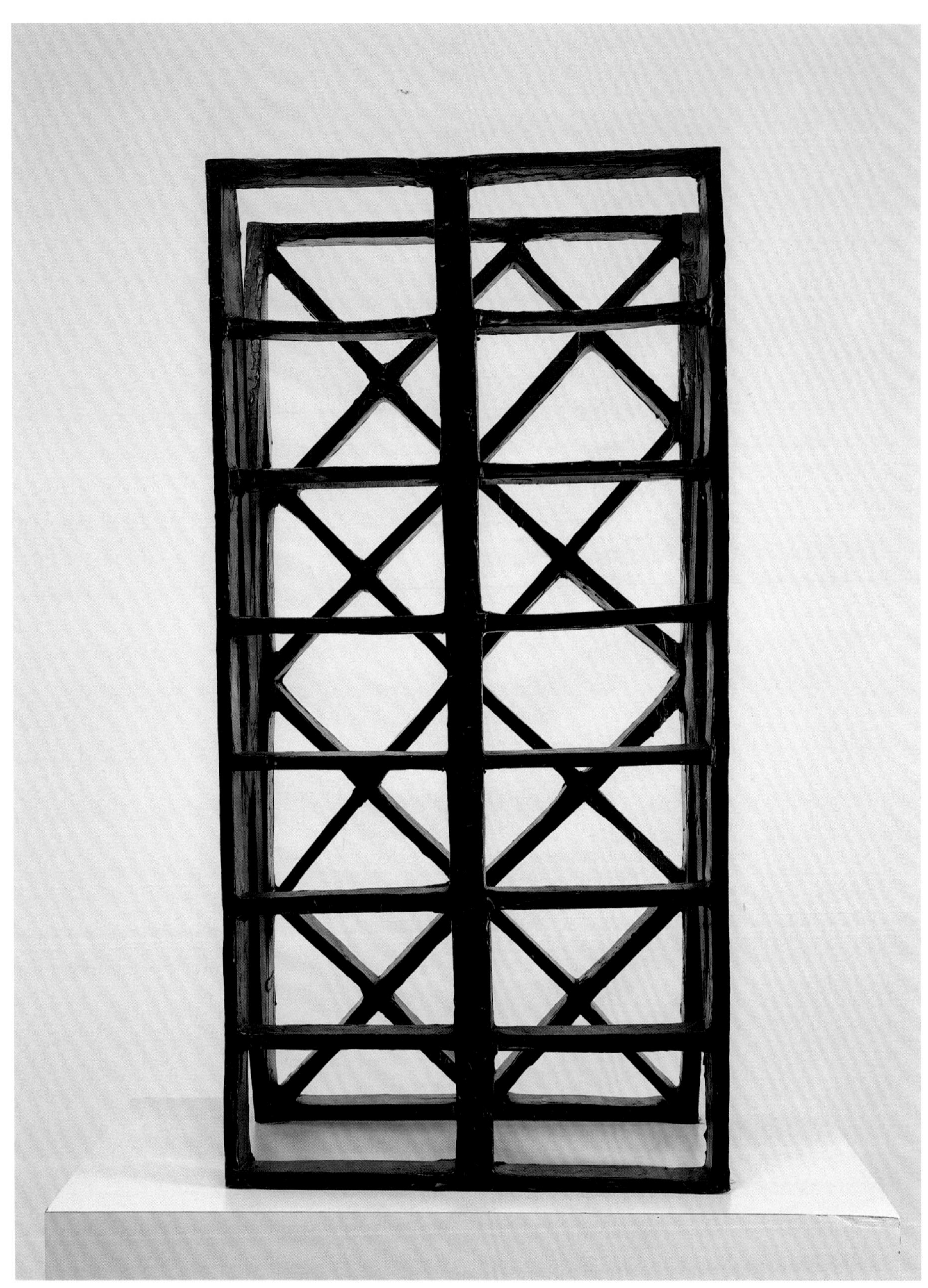

13. *But Twice*, 2003. Bronze, 32 x 16½ x 14 inches, edition of 6

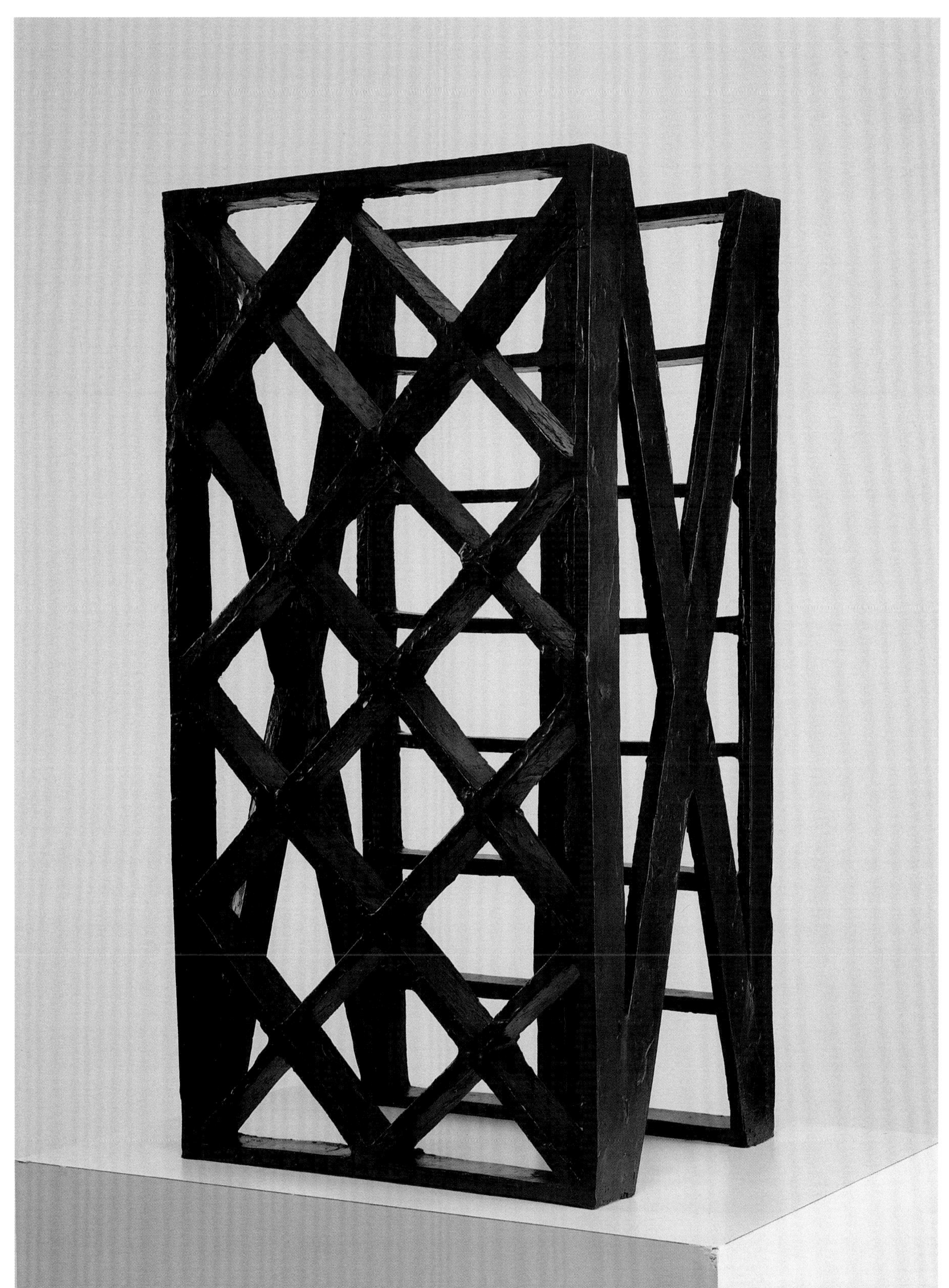

14. *In Pure Mind*, 2003. Bronze, 34 x 16 x 16 inches, edition of 6

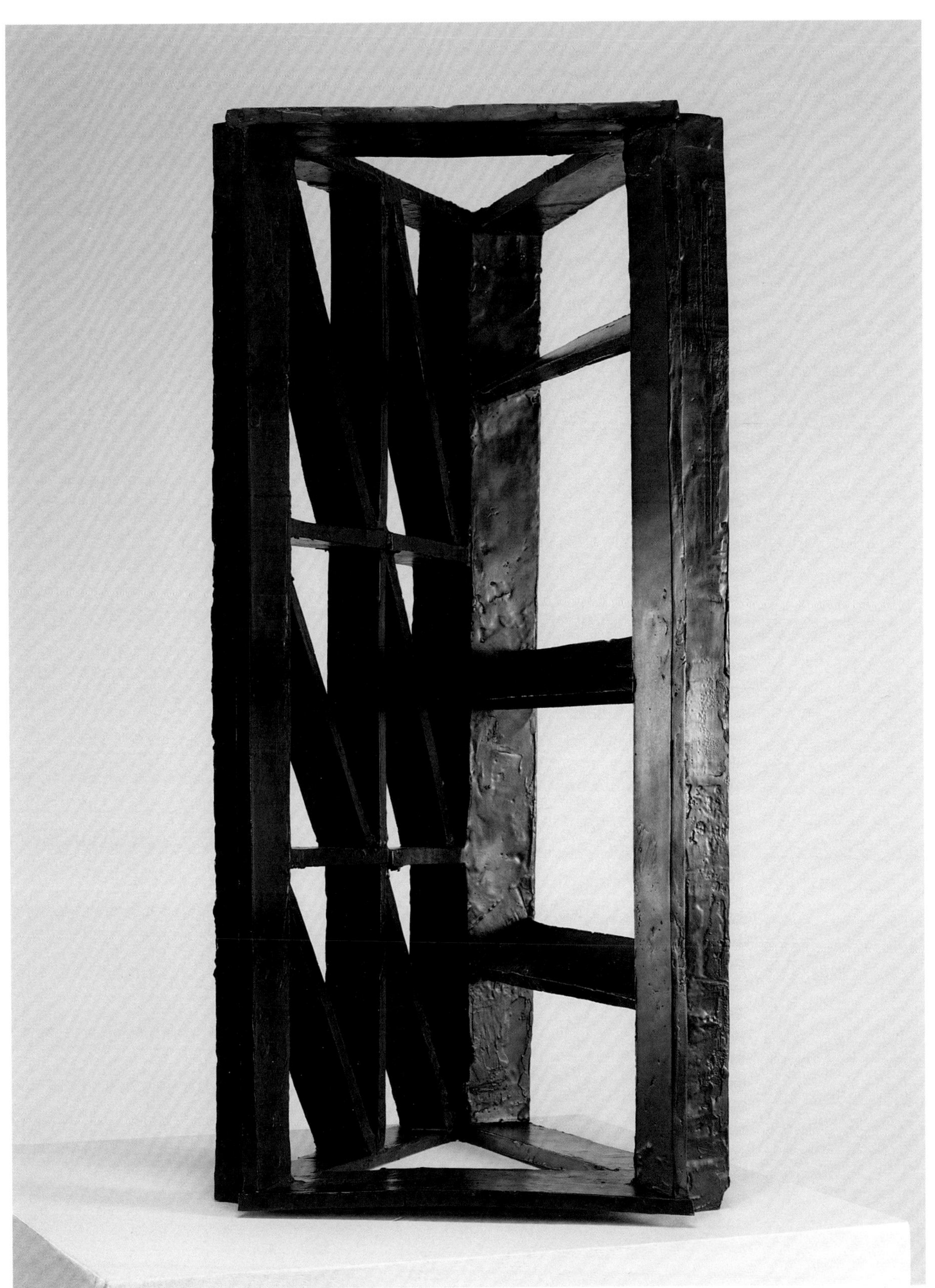

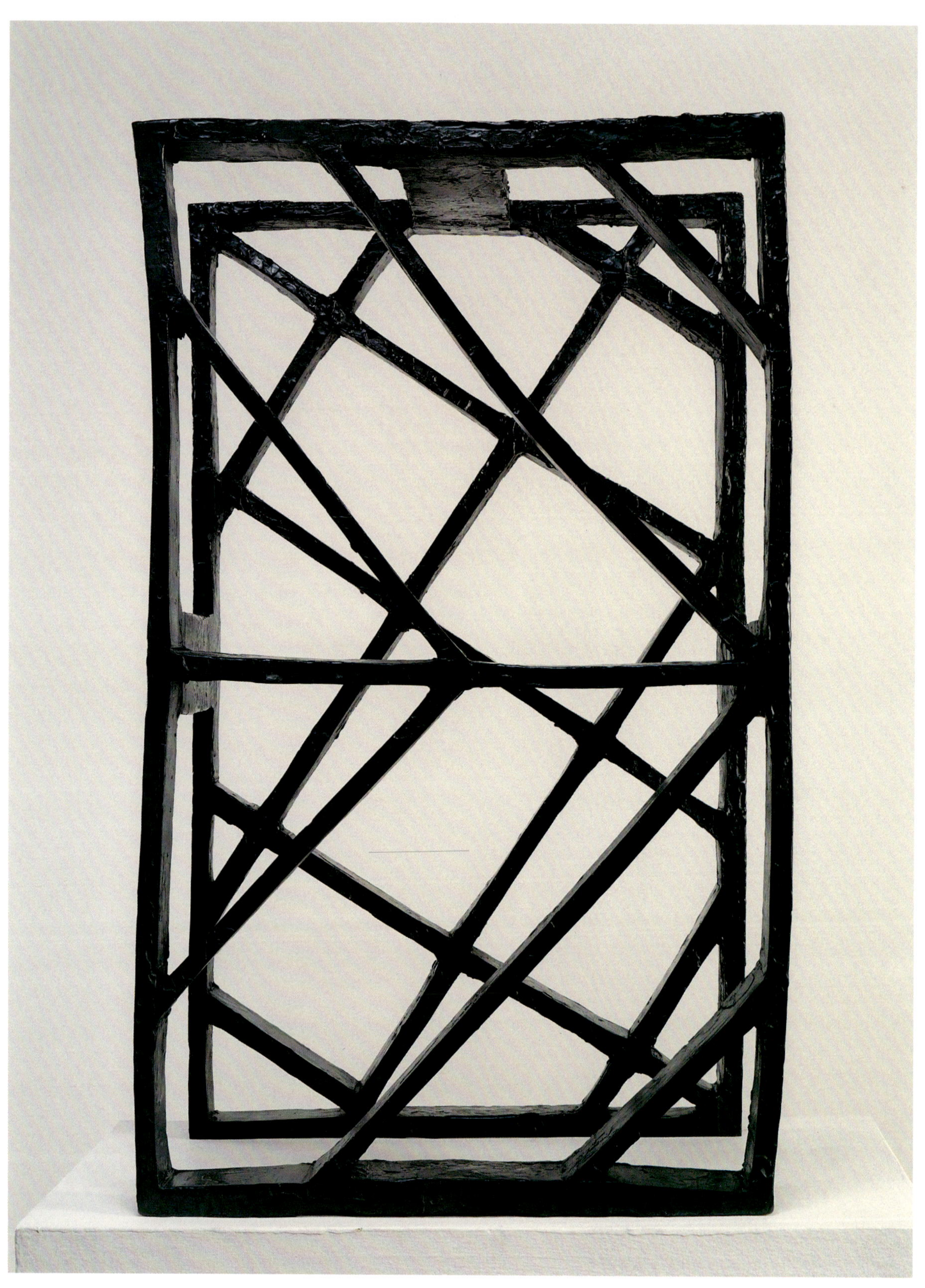

15. *Dance Undone*, 2003. Bronze, 30 x 13½ x 18 inches, edition of 6

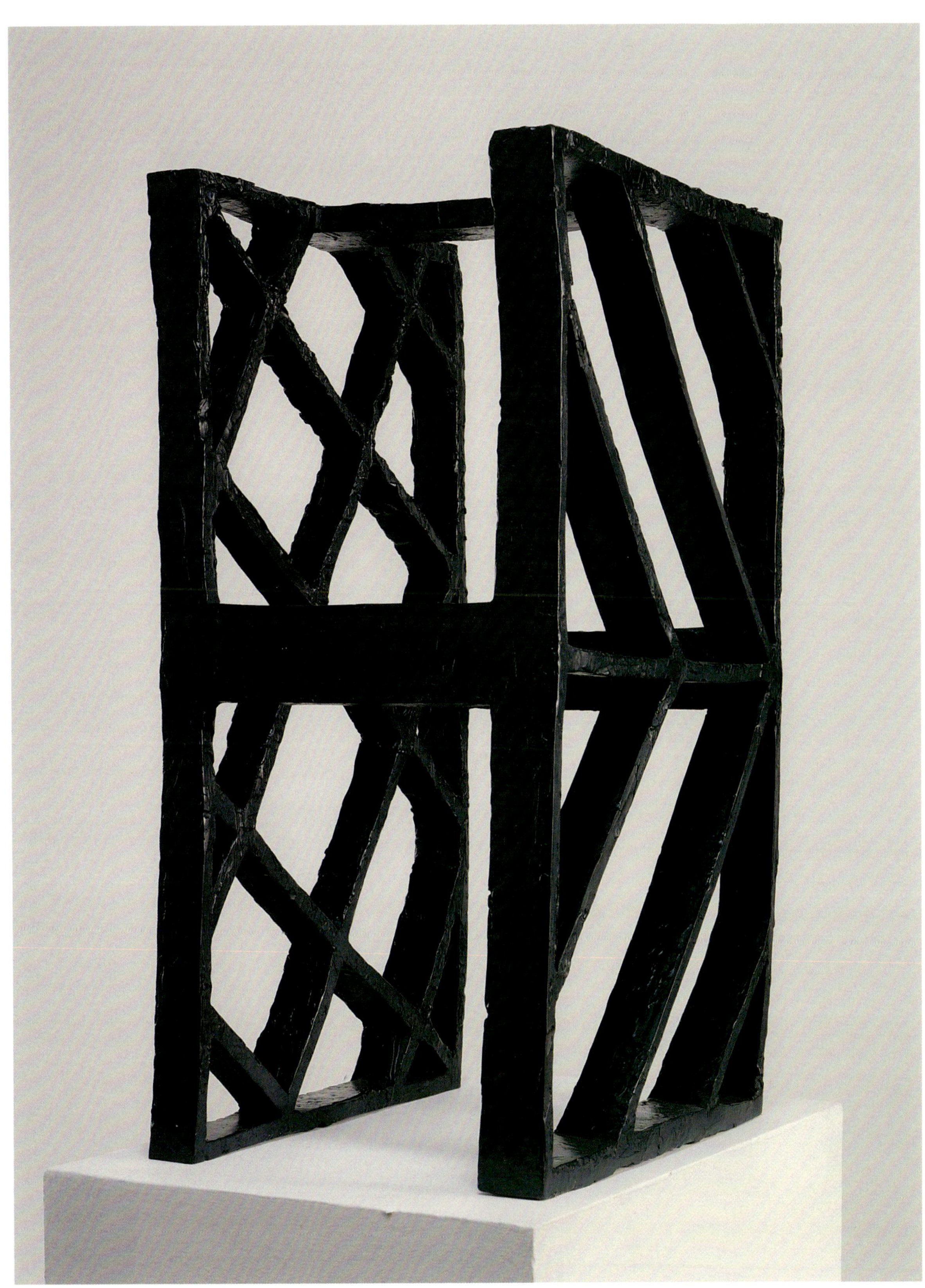

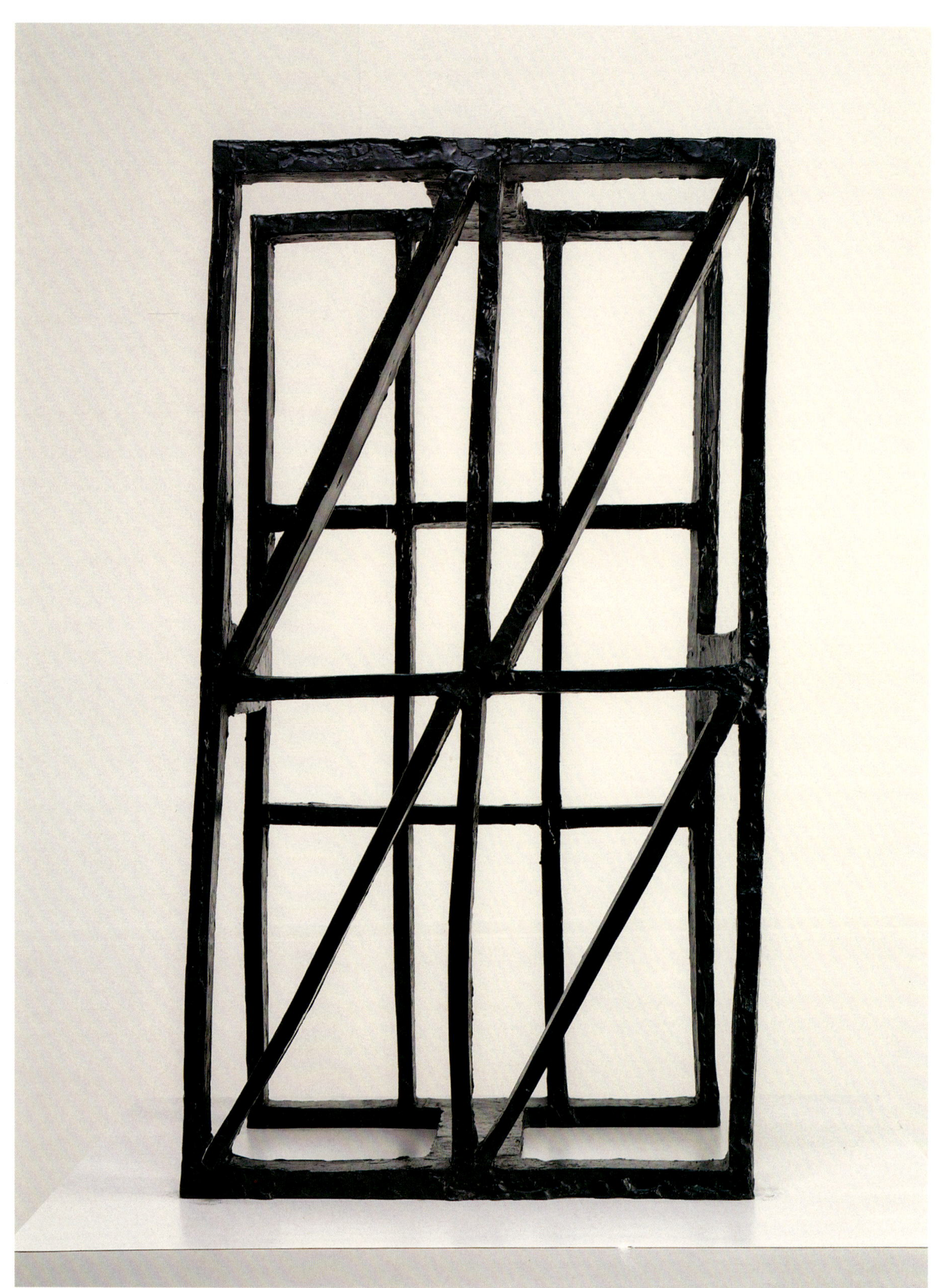

16. *Astraddle*, 2002. Bronze, 30 x 16¼ x 13 inches, edition of 6

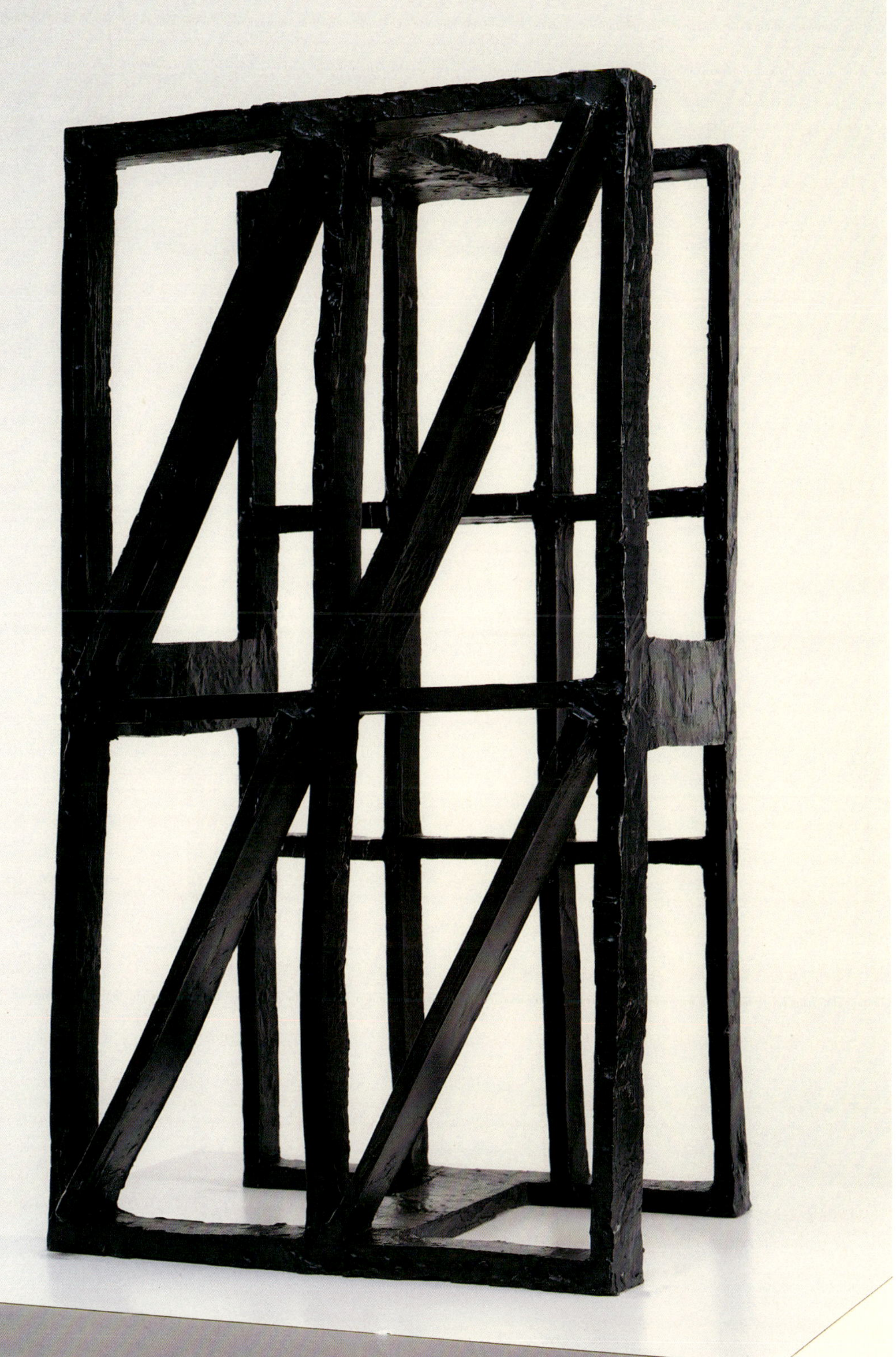

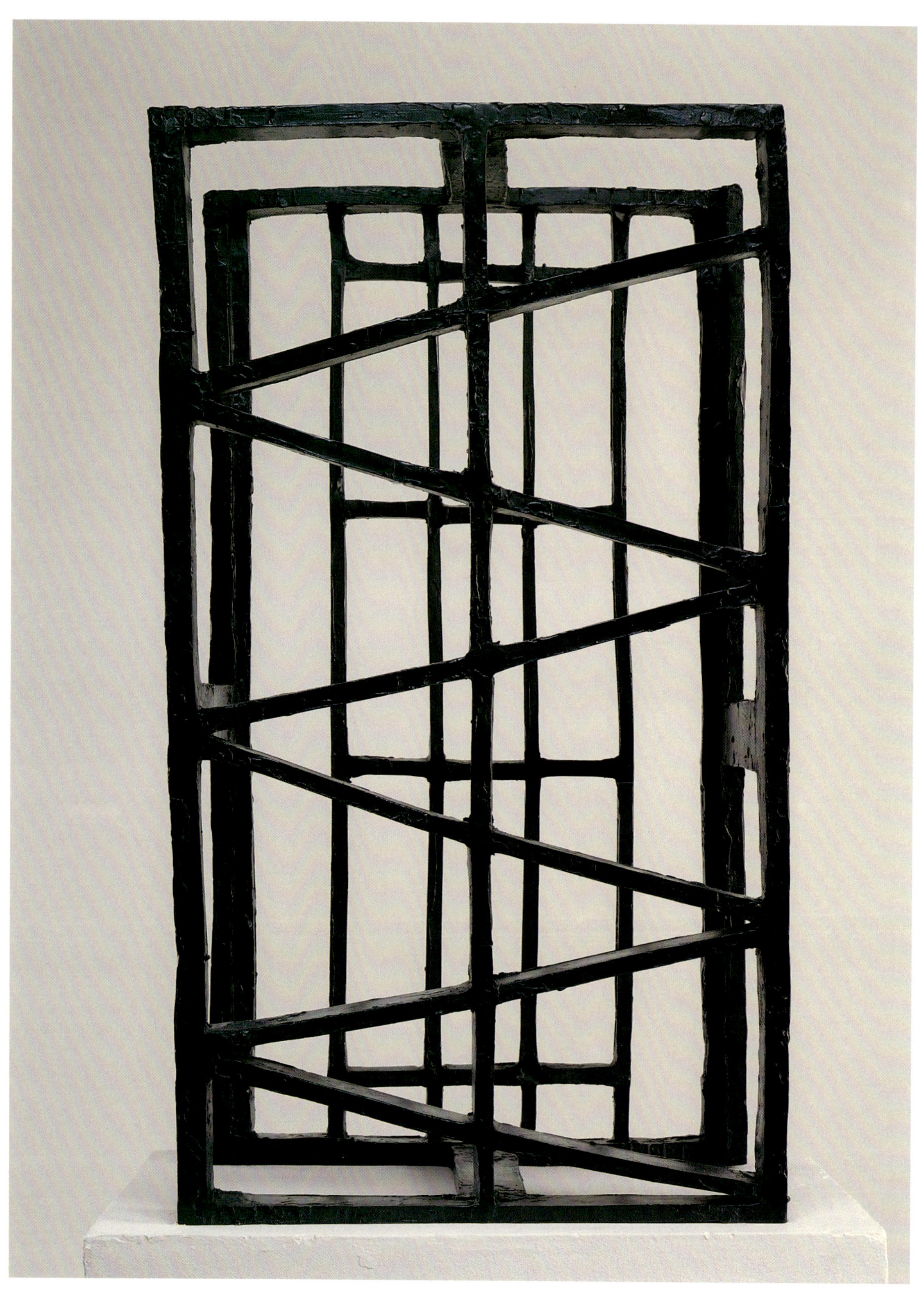

17. *Woven Sands*, 2002. Bronze, 33 x 19 x 15 inches, edition of 6

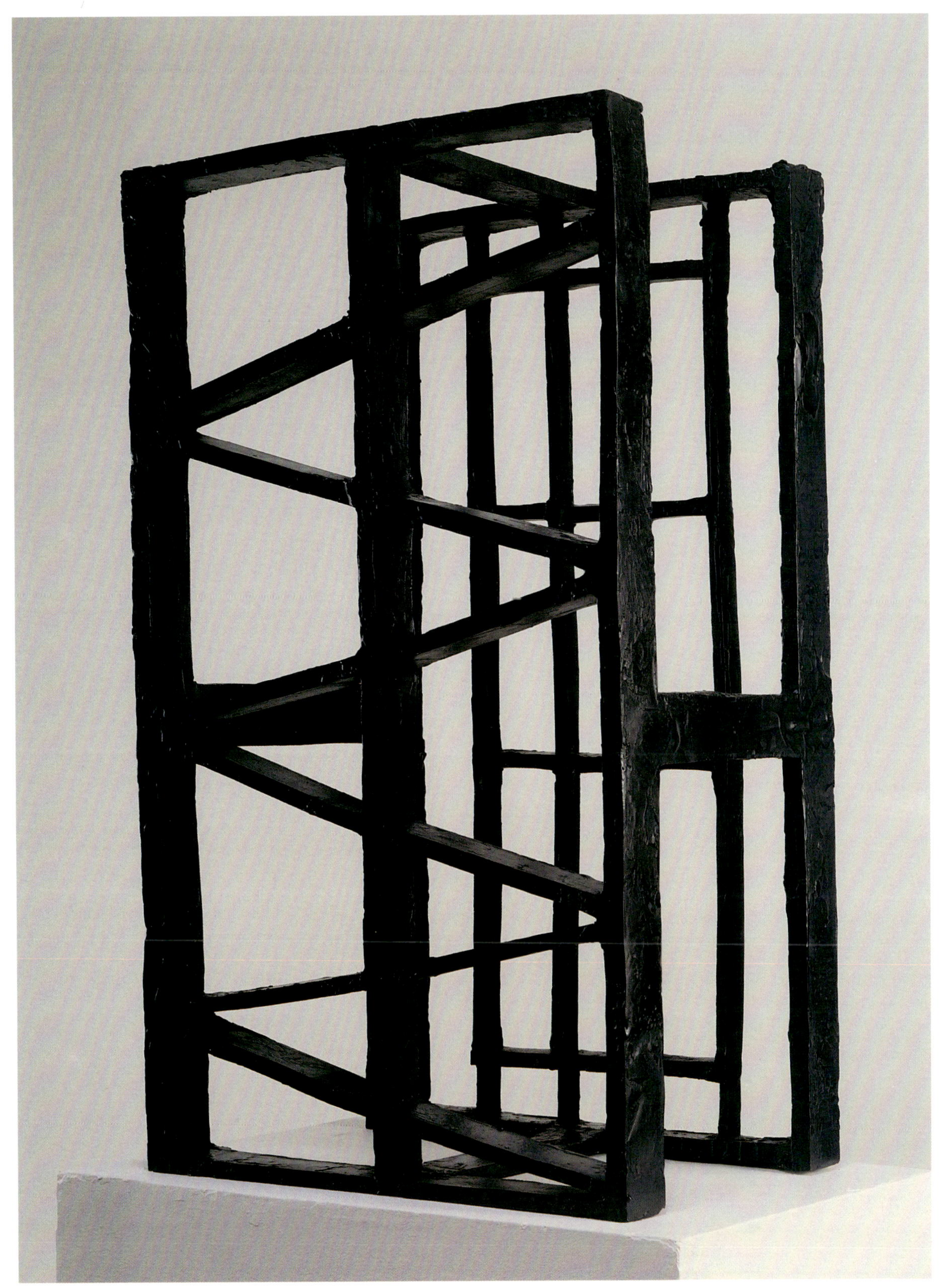

18. *Nine to Five*, 2002. Bronze, 35 x 17 x 9 inches, edition of 6

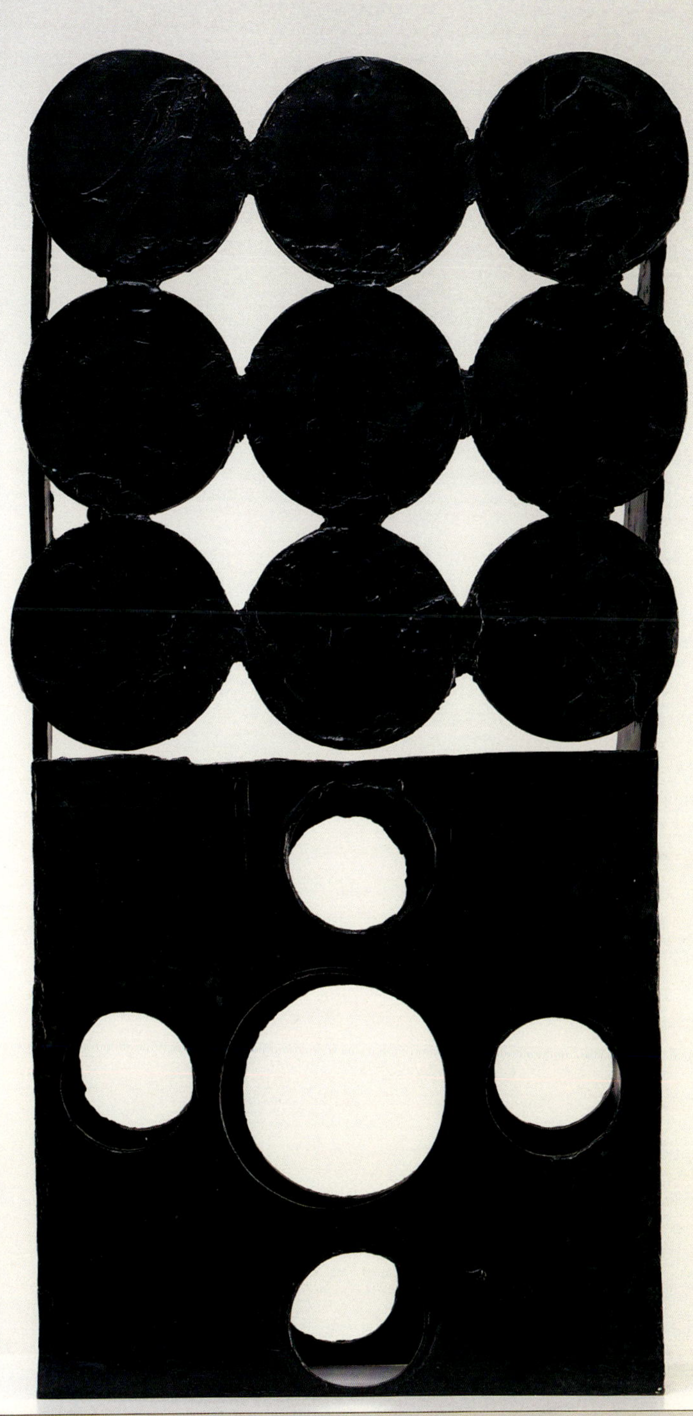

19. *Dow Star*, 2002. Bronze, 33½ x 14½ x 6 inches, edition of 6

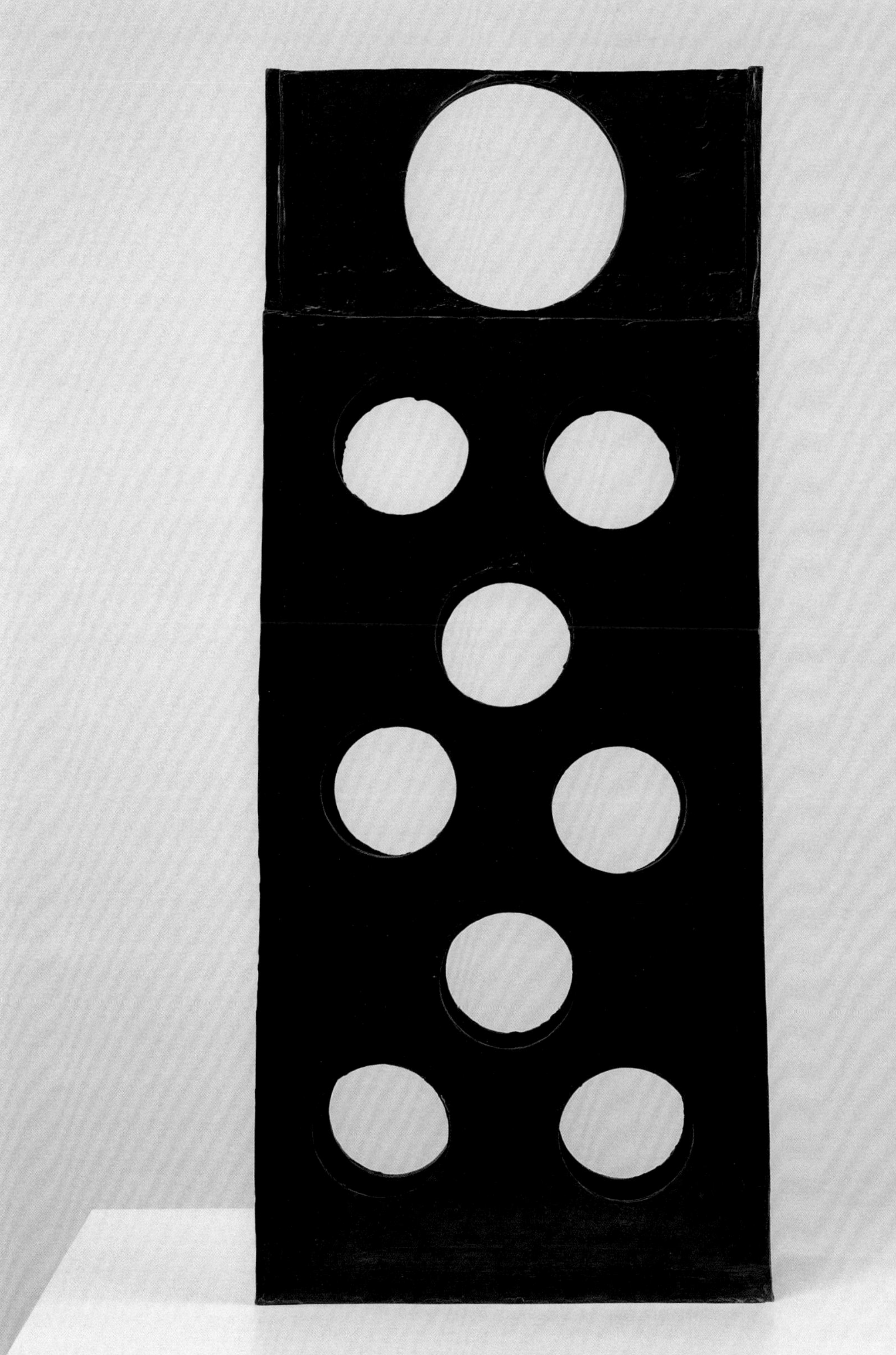

20. *Delicate Ear*, 2002. Bronze, 16¼ x 24½ x 12 inches, edition of 6

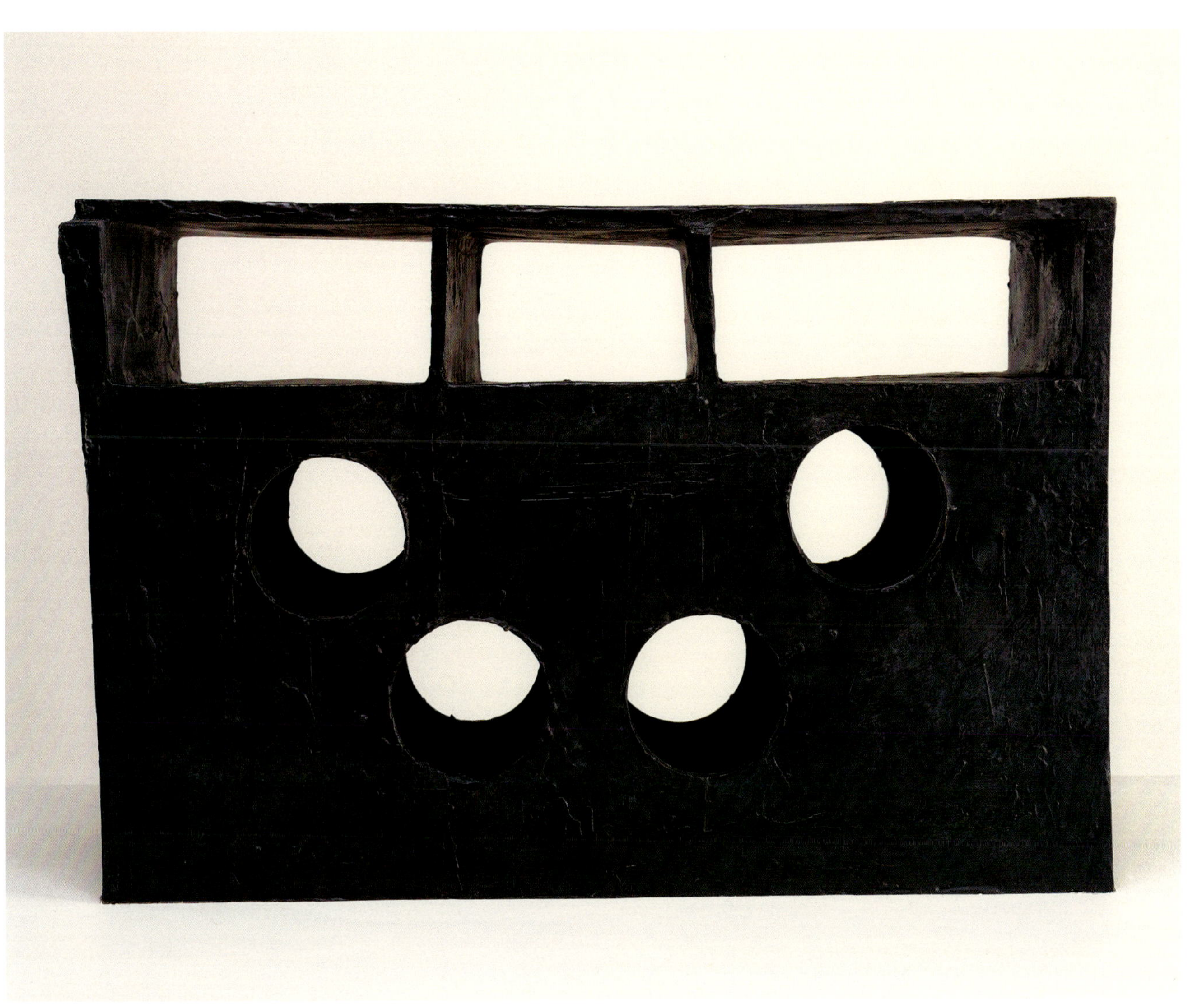

21. *Eros*, 2002. Bronze, 21½ x 31½ x 6 inches, edition of 6

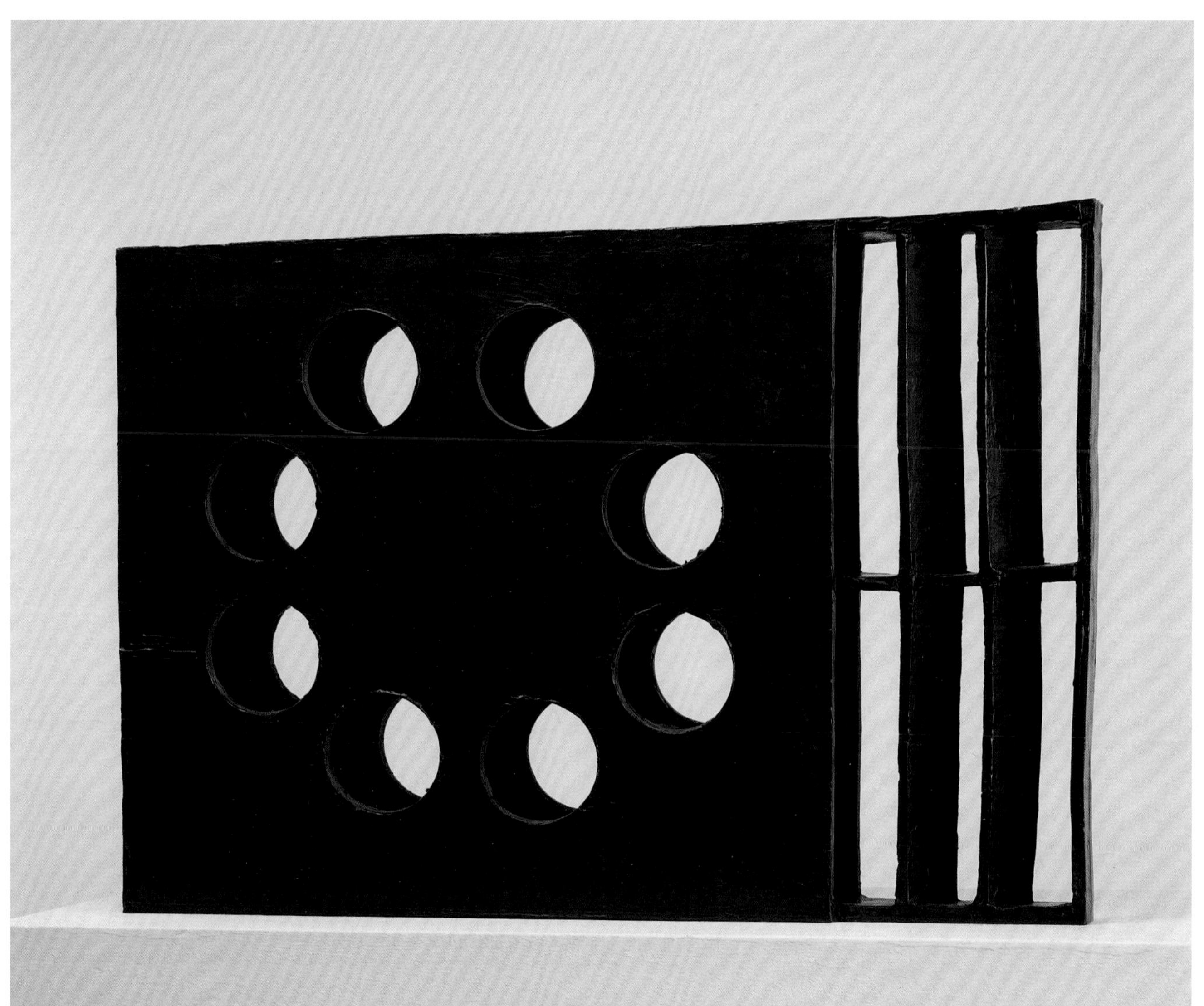

22. *Moonlit Dome*, 2002. Bronze, 32¼ x 22 x 11 inches, edition of 6

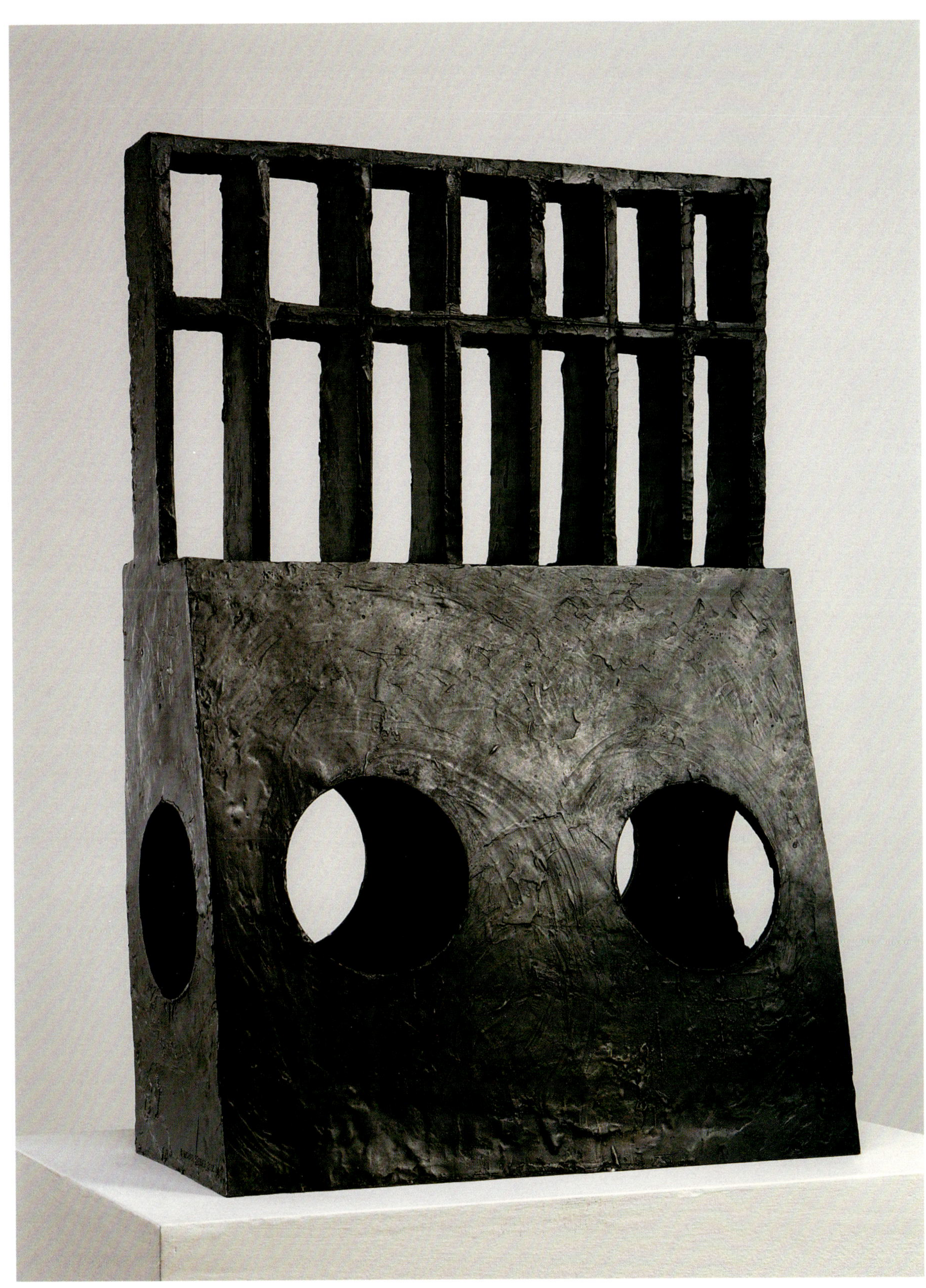

23. *Noiseless Sky*, 2002. Bronze, 26 x 24 x 14 inches, edition of 6

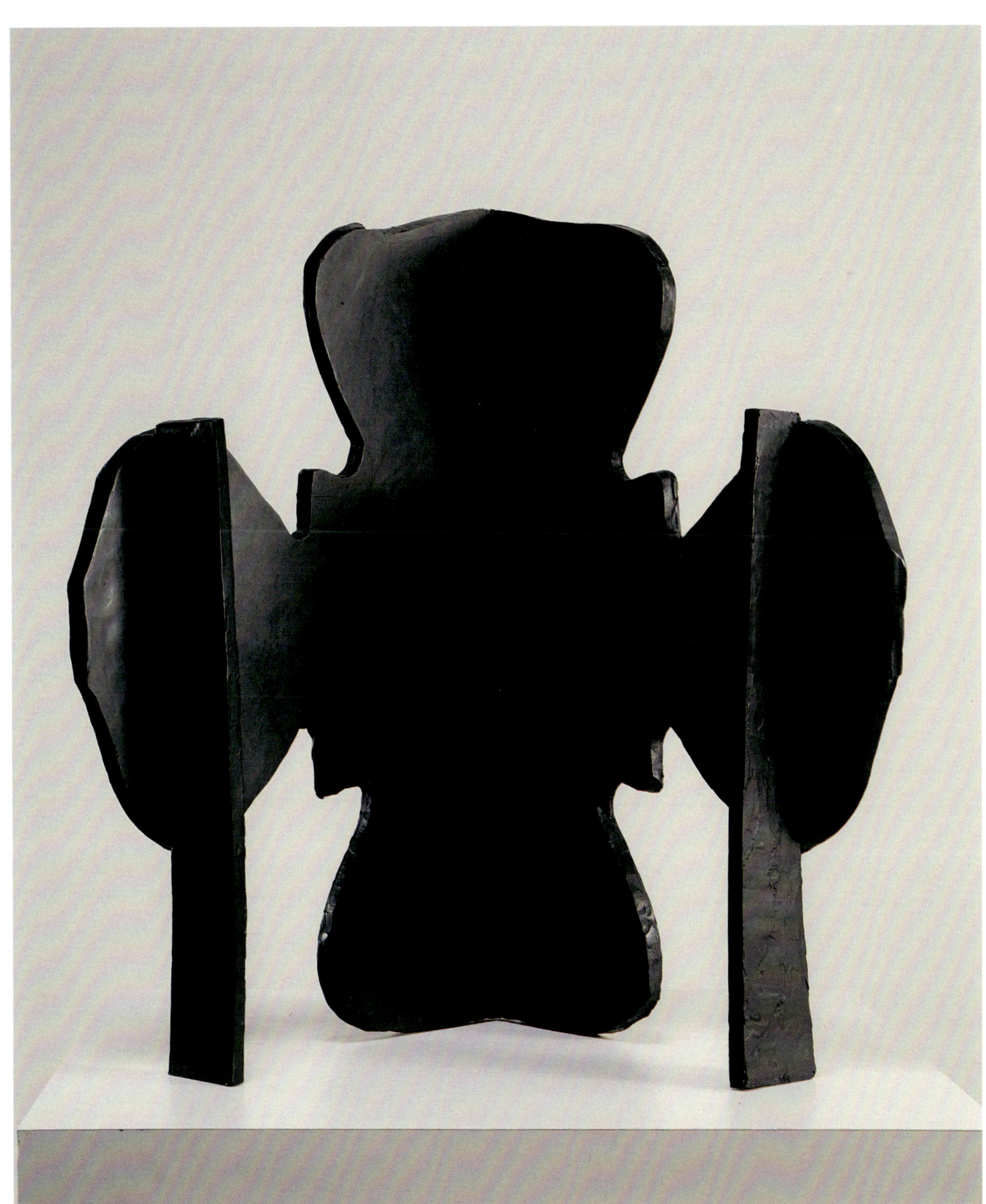

24. *Isis and Horus*, 2002. Bronze, 30 x 20 x 12 inches, edition of 6

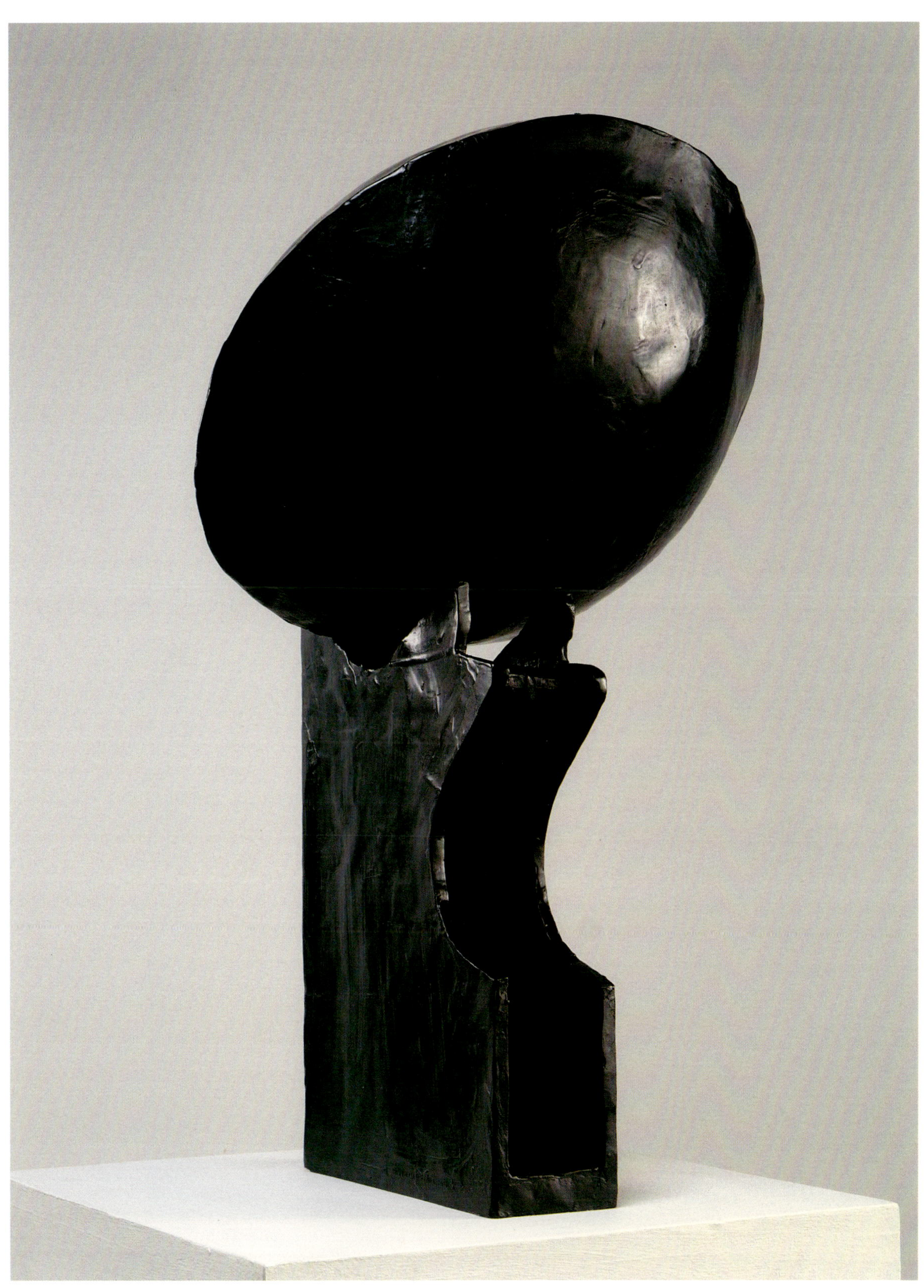

25. *Sept. 14, 2005*, 2005. Gouache, 60 x 40 inches

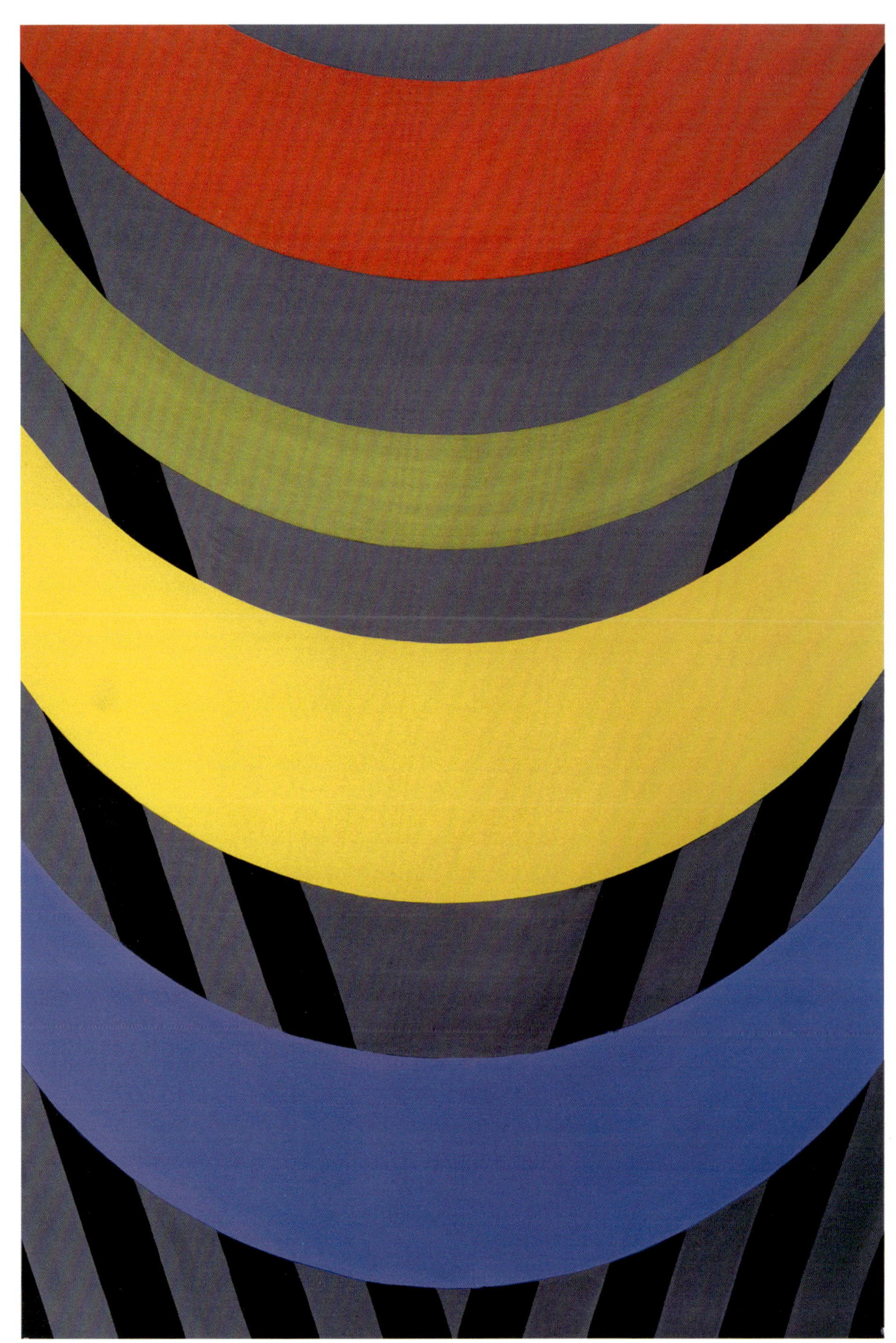

26. *Sept. 25, 2005*, 2005. Gouache, 60 x 40 inches

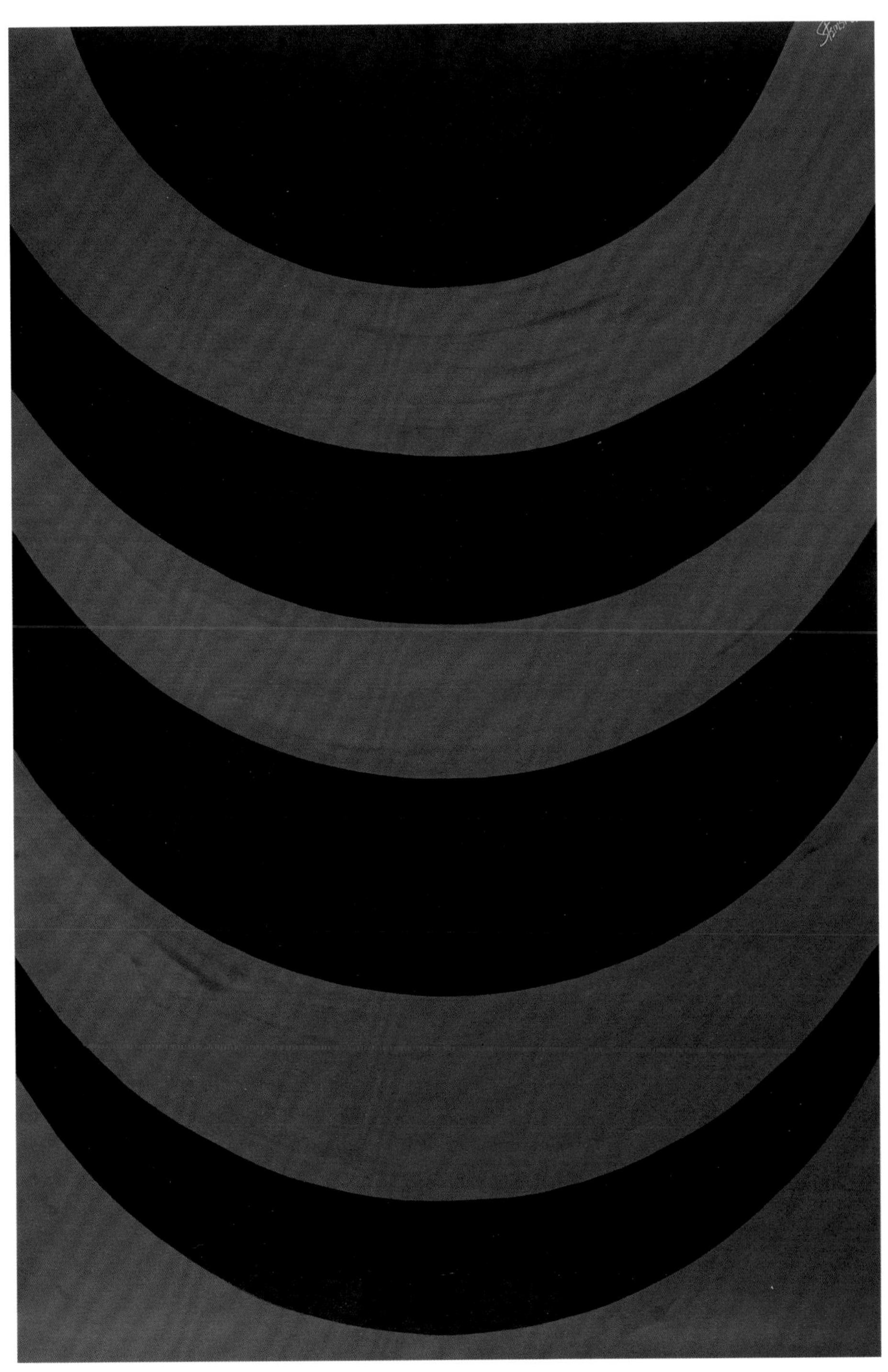

27. *Nov. 25, 2005*, 2005. Gouache, 60 x 40 inches

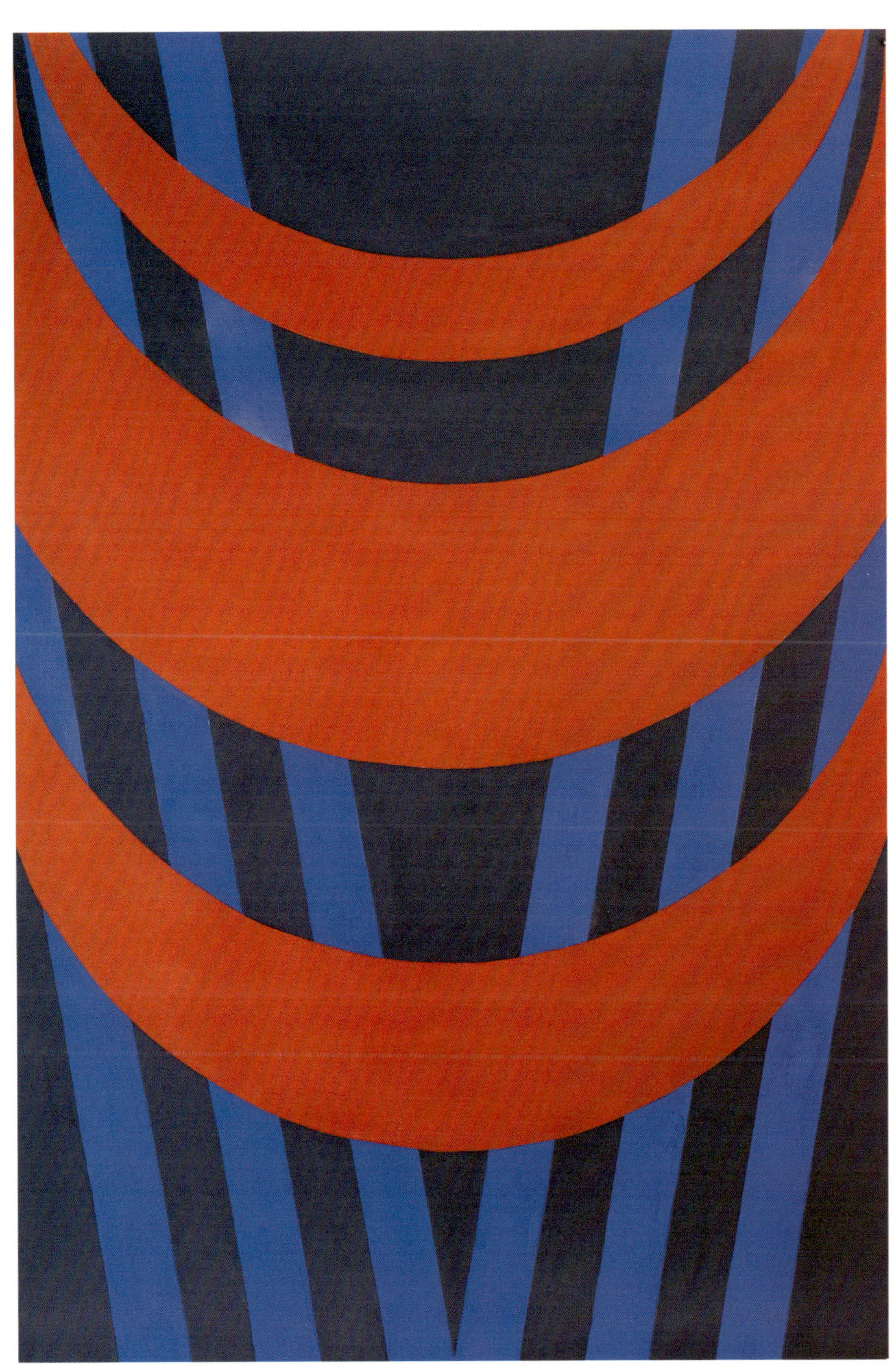

28. *Nov. 15, 2005,* 2005. Gouache, 60 x 40 inches

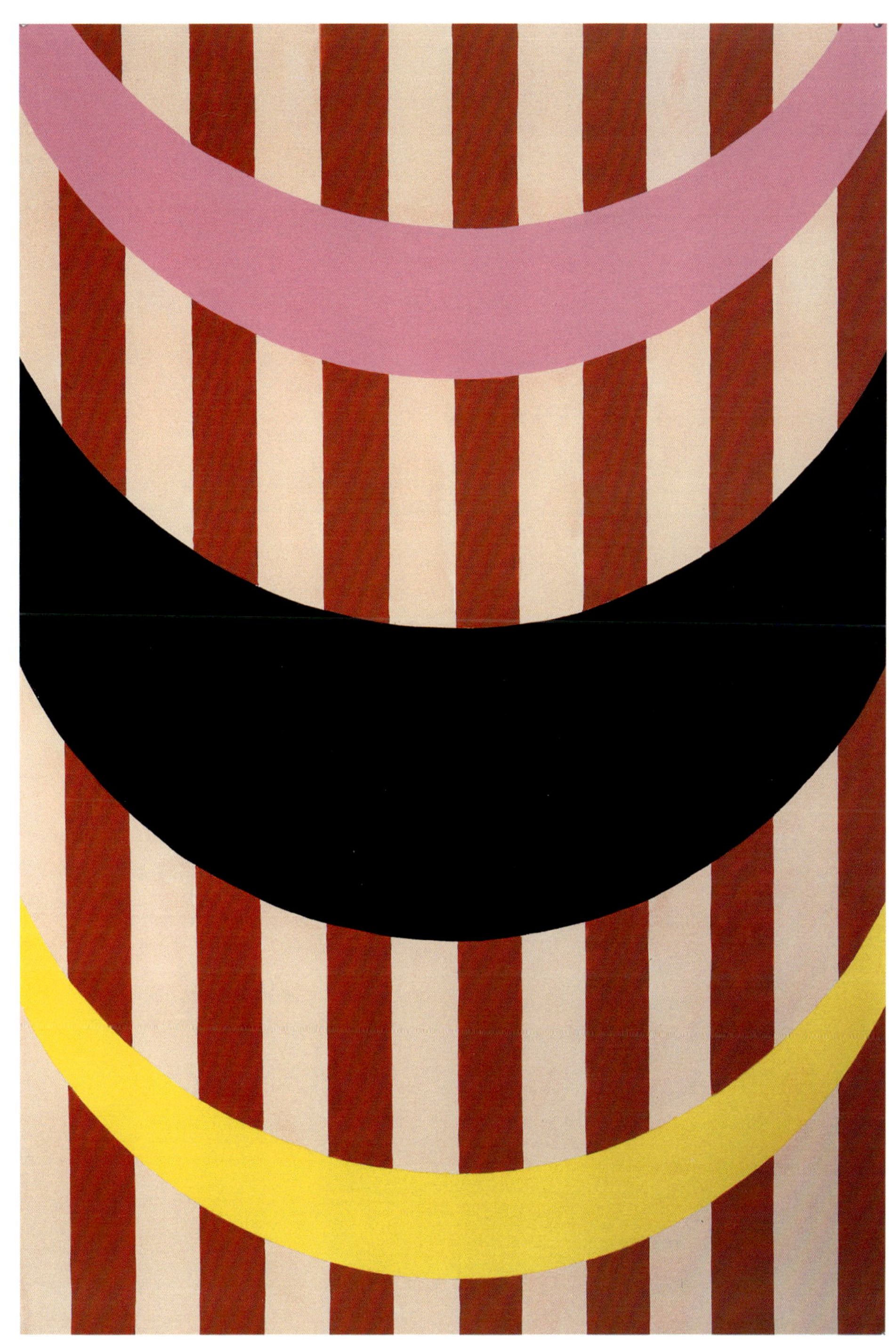

29. *Oct. 10, 2005*, 2005. Gouache, 60 x 40 inches

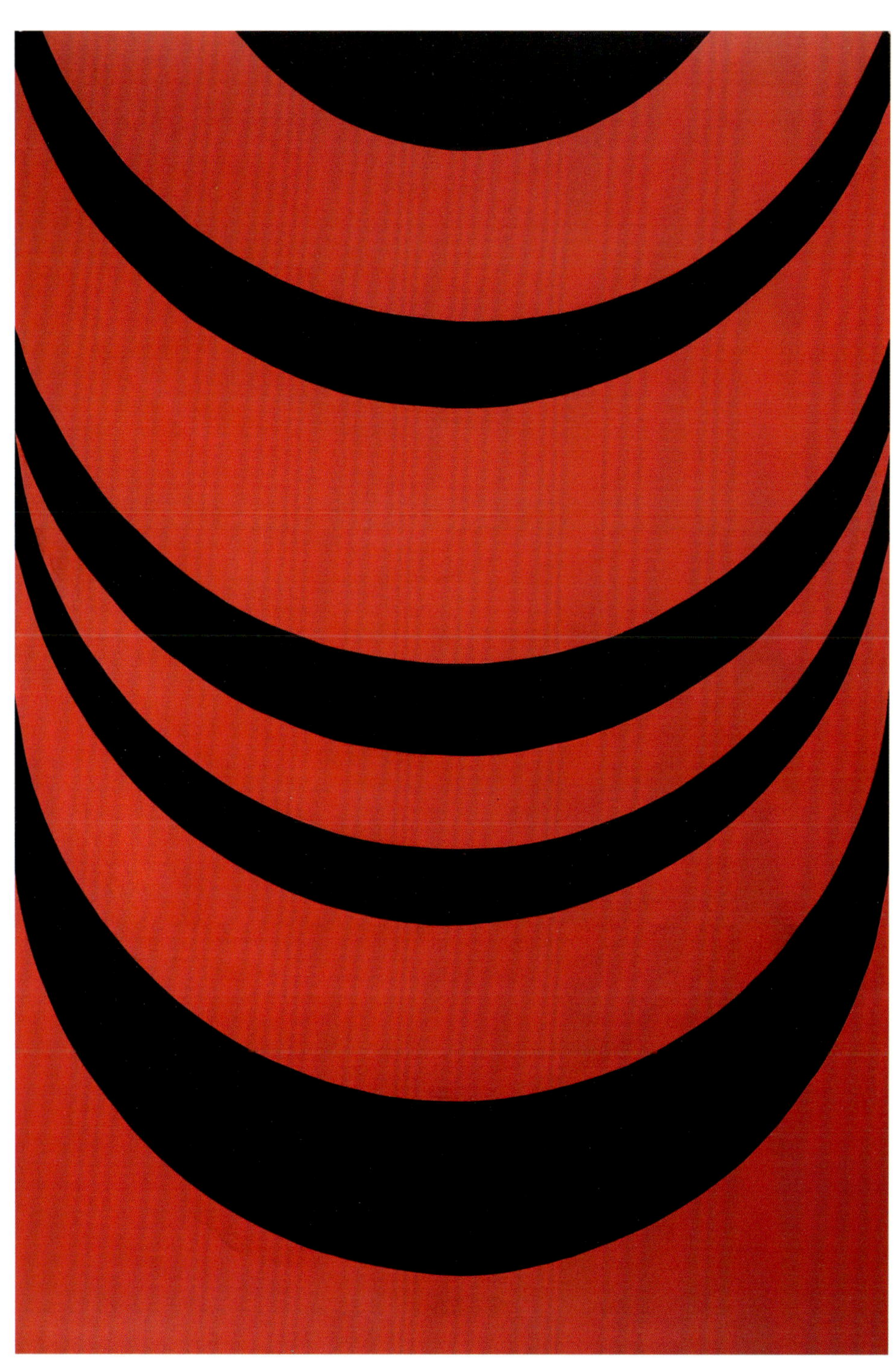

30. *Nov. 16, 2005,* 2005. Gouache, 60 x 40 inches

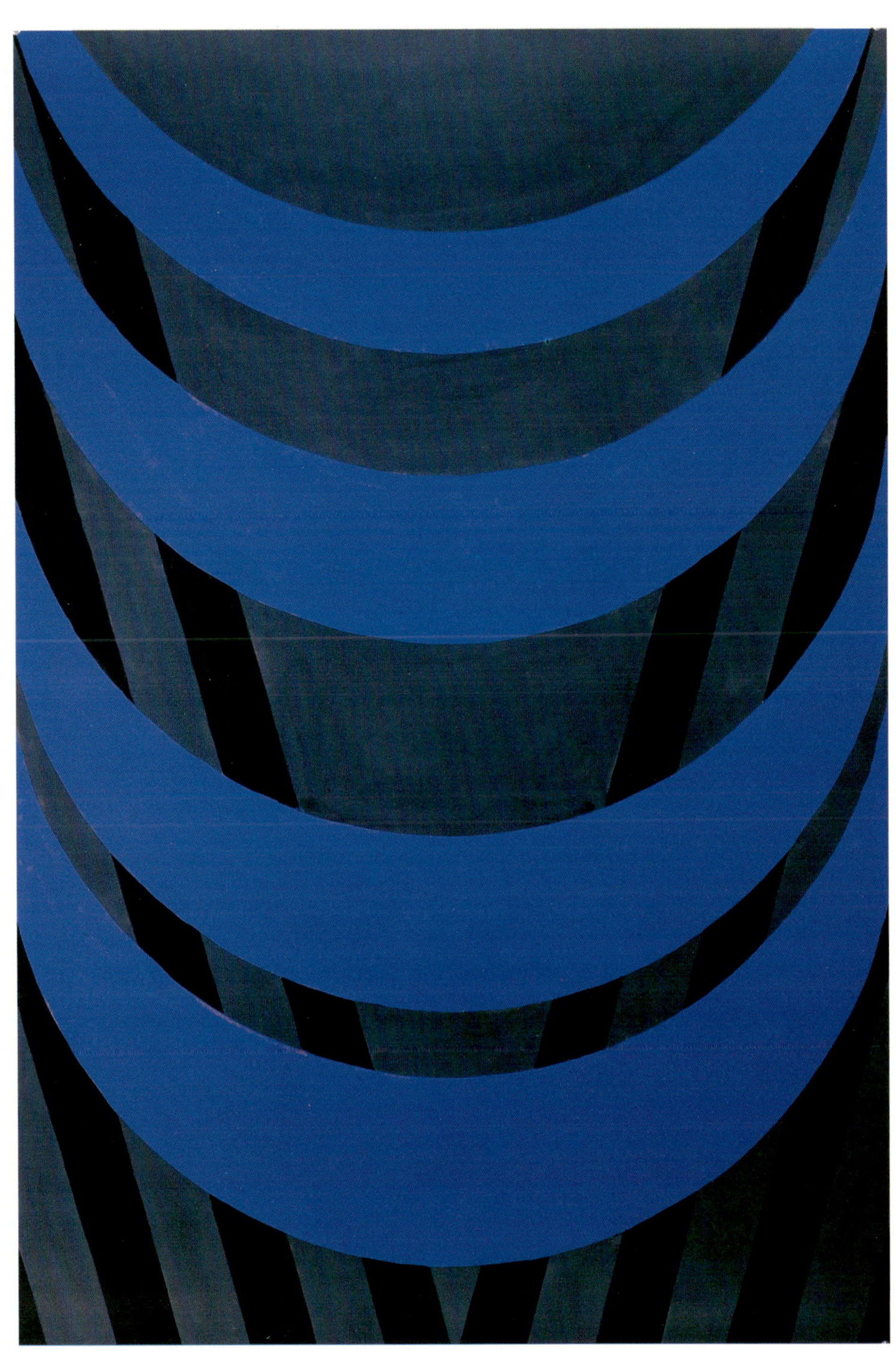

31. *Sept. 10, 2005,* 2005. Gouache, 60 x 40 inches

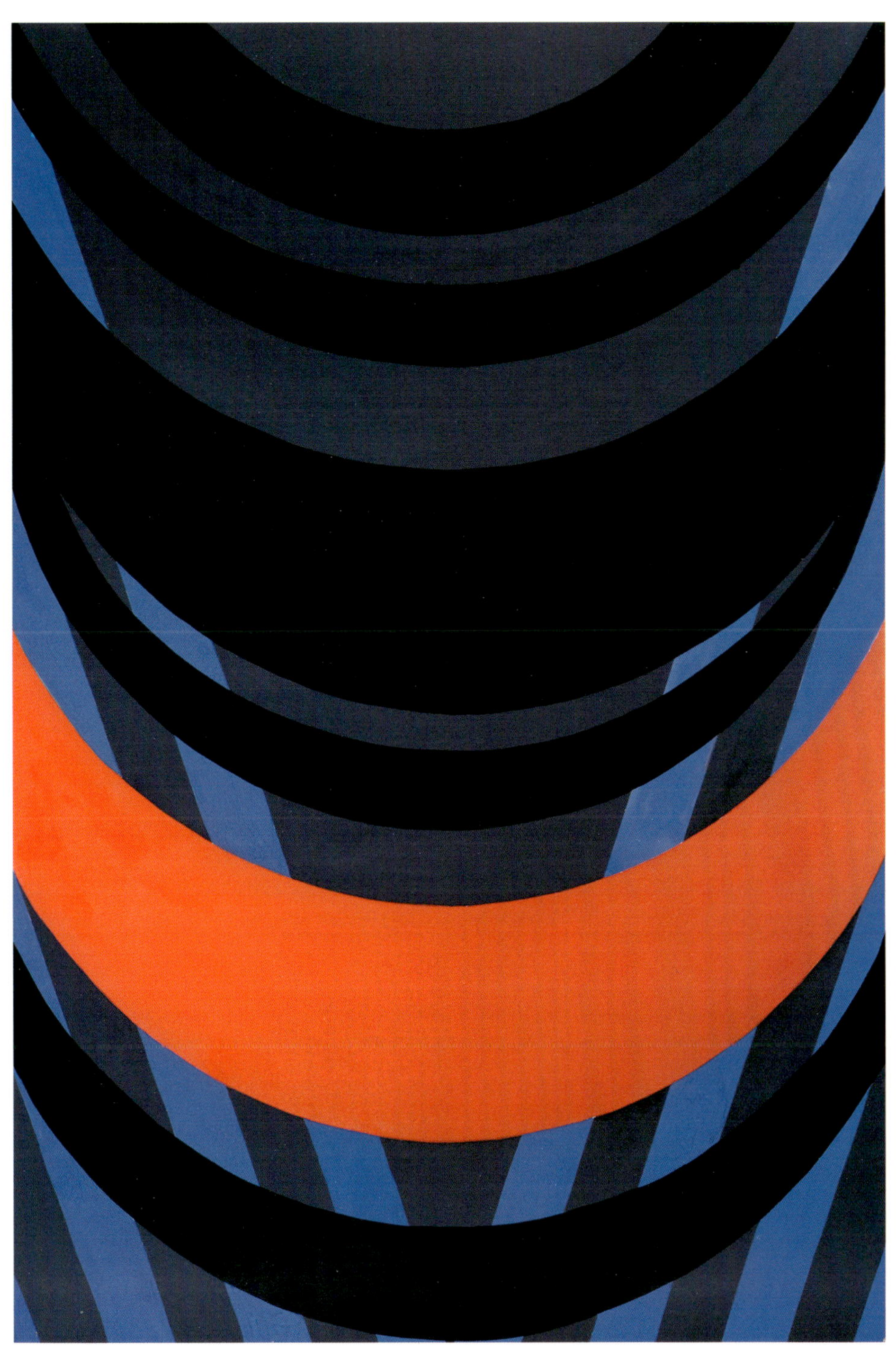

Michael Steiner
1945
Born, New York City
1971
Awarded Guggenheim Fellowship

ONE-PERSON EXHIBITIONS
1963
Fischbach Gallery, New York
1966
Dwan Gallery, New York
1968
Dwan Gallery, New York
1970
Norman Mackenzie Art Gallery, University of Saskatchewan,
    Regina, Canada
Marlborough Gallery, New York
Makler Gallery, Philadelphia, PA
David Mirvish Gallery, Toronto, Canada
1971
Hart House, University of Toronto, Canada
1972
Marlborough Gallery, New York
Noah Goldowsky/Richard Bellamy Gallery, New York
1974
Marlborough Gallery, New York
Museum of Fine Arts, Boston
1975
André Emmerich Gallery, New York
1976
Galerie Wentzel, Hamburg, Germany
David Mirvish Gallery, Toronto, Canada
André Emmerich Gallery, New York
1977
Kunsthalle, Bielefeld, Germany
Watson/de Nagy & Co., Houston, TX
Galerie André Emmerich, Zurich, Switzerland
Harcus-Krakow Gallery, Boston, MA
1978
André Emmerich Gallery, New York
David Mirvish Gallery, Toronto, Ontario, Canada
Galerie Gerald Piltzer, Paris, France
Kunst-und-Museumsverein, Wuppertal, Germany
1979
André Emmerich Gallery, New York
Galerie Wentzel, Hamburg, Germany
Amerika Haus, Berlin, Germany
Galerie Tiergarten, Hannover, Germany
Harcus-Krakow Gallery, Boston
1980
Galerie Ninety-Nine, Bay Harbor Islands, FL
André Emmerich Gallery, New York
Meredith Long & Co., New York
1981
Galerie Wentzel, Hamburg, Germany
André Emmerich Gallery, New York
Meredith Long & Co., Houston, TX
Gallery One, Toronto, Canada
1982
André Emmerich Gallery, New York
The Hett Gallery Ltd., Edmonton, Alberta, Canada
Galerie Wentzel, Cologne, West Germany
Barbara Balkin Gallery, Chicago
Harcus-Krakow Gallery, Boston

1983
André Emmerich Gallery, New York
Martha White Gallery, Louisville, KY
1985
Galerie Elca London, Montreal, Quebec, Canada
Douglas Drake Gallery, Kansas City, KS
André Emmerich Gallery, New York
Meredith Long & Co., Houston, TX
1987
André Emmerich Gallery, New York
1990
Salander-O'Reilly Galleries, New York
Helander Gallery, Palm Beach, FL
1992
Museum of Art, Fort Lauderdale, FL ("Drawings and Bronzes"
    and "Monumental Sculpture")
Salander-O'Reilly Galleries, New York
1993
Galerie Gerald Piltzer, Paris
Salander-O'Reilly Galleries, New York
1994
Schulte Gallery, Millburn, NJ
1995
Salander-O'Reilly Galleries, New York
1997
Salander-O'Reilly Galleries, New York
1998
Schulte Gallery, Millburn, NJ
Grounds For Sculpture, Hamilton, NJ
1999
Salander-O'Reilly Galleries, New York
2000
Galerie Piltzer, Paris
2001
Salander-O'Reilly Galleries, New York
2003
Salander-O'Reilly Galleries, New York
2005
Yellow Bird, Newburgh, NY
2006
Salander-O'Reilly Galleries, New York

SELECTED GROUP EXHIBITIONS
1964
Light Show, Institute of Contemporary Art, Philadelphia, PA
1965
Box Show, Byron Gallery, New York
1966
Gallery Group, Dwan Gallery, New York
The Ten, Dwan Gallery, New York
1968
Larry Aldrich Museum of Contemporary Art, Ridgefield, CT
Minimal Art, Gemeentemuseum, The Hague
8 American Sculptors, Pioneer Court, Chicago, IL
1969
Marlborough-Gerson Gallery, New York
1970
Annual Exhibition: Contemporary American Sculpture,
    Whitney Museum of American Art, New York
Contemporary Painting and Sculpture, Jewett Arts Center,
    Wellesley College, Wellesley, MA
The Form of Color, Toledo Museum of Art, OH
The Philadelphia Art Alliance, Philadelphia, PA
Marlborough Gallery, New York

1971
The de Luxe Show, Houston, TX
Sculpture in the Park, Van Saun Park, Paramus, NJ
20th Century Sculpture, Akron Art Institute, OH
1972
20th Century Sculpture, Contemporary Art Center, Cincinnati, OH
Masters of the Sixties, Edmonton Art Gallery and Winnipeg Art
     Gallery, Canada
The Gosman Collection, University of Michigan Museum of Art,
     Ann Arbor, MI
Biennial Exhibition: Contemporary American Art, Whitney
     Museum of American Art, New York
1973
Emma Lake Artists, Norman Mackenzie Art Gallery, University of
     Saskatchewan, Regina, Canada
11 Americans, Museum of Contemporary Art, Montreal,
1974
Twentieth Century Monumental Sculpture, Marlborough Gallery,
     New York
Sculpture in Steel, The Edmonton Art Gallery, Edmonton, Alberta,
     Canada; David Mirvish Gallery, Toronto, Ontario, Canada
1975
Early Years, The School of Visual Arts, New York
The Condition of Sculpture, The Arts Council of Great Britain,
     Hayward Gallery, London
National Institute of Arts and Letters, New York
Art Works, Milwaukee, Wisconsin
1976
New Works in Clay by Contemporary Painters and Sculptors, Everson
     Museum of Art, Syracuse; Edmonton Art Gallery, Edmonton,
     Alberta, Canada
1977
Eighteen Contemporary Masters, United States Embassy, Ottawa,
     Canada
1978
ART 9/78, Basel, Switzerland
Skulpturen und Gemälde aus New York, Kunst-und-Museumsverein,
     Wuppertal, Germany
1979
A Century of Ceramics in the United States, 1878–1978, Everson
     Museum of Art, Syracuse, NY; Renwick Gallery of the National
     Collection of Fine Arts, Smithsonian Institution, Washington,
     DC; Cooper-Hewitt Museum, New York
1980
Gonzalez, Smith, Caro, Scott, Steiner, Galerie de France, Paris;
     Kunsthalle Bielefeld; Haus am Waldsee, Berlin; Kunsthalle
     Tubingen; Galerie Wentzel, Hamburg; Wilhelm-Hack-Museum,
     Ludwigshafen
L'Amérique aux Indépendants, 91e Exposition, Société des Artistes,
     Grand Palais, Paris
In the Constructivist Spirit/1980, Janus Gallery, Venice, CA
Works on Paper, Allen Rubiner Gallery, Royal Oak, MI
Contemporary Works on Paper, Meredith Long & Co.,
     Houston, TX
All in Line: An Exhibition of Linear Drawing, Joe and Emily Lowe
     Art Gallery, Syracuse University, Syracuse, NY, November 23,
     1980–January 18, 1981; Terry Dintenfass, NY, January, 31–February
     27, 1981
1981
Uniquely Painted Prints, Salander-O'Reilly Galleries, Inc., New York
Sculpture Selection I, Salander-O'Reilly Galleries, Inc., New York
Skulptur Begreifen, Museum Sprengel, Hannover, Germany
Bildhauertechniken, Dimension des Plastischen, Staatliche Kunsthalle,
     Berlin, Germany

1982
Casting: A Survey of Cast Metal Sculpture in the 80s, Fuller Goldeen
     Gallery, San Francisco, CA
New Small Sculpture, The Edmonton Gallery, Edmonton, Alberta,
     Canada
1983
Bronze at Washington Square, The Public Art Trust, Washington, DC
André Emmerich Gallery, New York
1984
Arte Contemporaneo Norteamerican, Colleccion David Mirvish,
     American Embassy in Madrid, January
Transformations, Katonah Gallery, Katonah, NY
Seven Sculptors, André Emmerich Gallery, New York
Works in Bronze: A Modern Survey, traveling exhibition scheduled
     from 1984–1986: University Art Gallery, Sonoma State University,
     Rohnert Park, CA, November 2–December 16, 1984; Redding
     Museum and Art Center, Redding, CA, May 1–June 2, 1985;
     University Art Gallery, Fresno State University Fresno, CA,
     September 1–October 20, 1985; Palm Springs Desert Museum,
     Palm Springs, CA, November 15, 1985–January 12, 1986; Boise
     Gallery of Art, Boise, ID, February 21–March 30, 1986; Cheney
     Cowles Memorial Museum, Eastern Washington State Historical
     Society, April 24–June 1, 1986; University Art Gallery, California
     State University, Stanislaus, CA, September–October 1986;
     University of CA, Santa Cruz, CA, November–December 1986
1985
Pre Postmodern, The Richard F. Brush Art Gallery, St. Lawrence
     University, Canton, NY
Selections from the William J. Hokin Collection, Museum of
     Contemporary Art, Chicago, IL
Six Sculptors, André Emmerich Gallery, New York
1986
Works in Bronze, Sierra Nevada Museum of Art, Reno, NV
1987
Works on Paper, The Alpha Gallery, Boston, MA
1988
Contemporary Abstract Sculpture, Carl Schlosberg Fine Arts,
     Sherman Oaks, CA
1989
For the Collector: Important Contemporary Sculpture, Meredith Long
     & Co., Houston, TX
1989 Bruce Museum Connecticut Biennial, The Bruce Museum,
     Greenwich, CT
Important Works on Paper, Meredith Long & Co.
Sculptural Intimacies: Recent Small-Scale Work, Security Pacific
     Gallery, South Coast Metro Center, Costa Mesa, CA
1990
Group: 1990, Salander-O'Reilly Galleries, New York
Grounded: Sculpture on the Floor, The University of Michigan
     Museum of Art
Reflections and Mirror Images, Steven Scott Gallery, Baltimore, MD
New Abstraction: Recent Painting, Sound Shore Gallery, Stamford, CT
1991
Gallery Selections, Salander-O'Reilly Galleries, New York
Inaugural Exhibition, Salander-O'Reilly Galleries, Berlin, Germany
1992
Celebrating Formalsim, Schulte Gallery, Millburn, NJ
1993
The Invitational Exhibition of Paintings and Sculpture, American
     Academy and Institute of Arts & Letters
Important Works by Modern Masters, Schulte Gallery, Millburn, NJ
1995
Selection of Bronze Sculpture, Salander-O'Reilly Galleries,
     New York

Tampa Museum of Art, Tampa, Florida
1999
Recent Sculpture, Salander-O'Reilly Galleries, New York
2001
Pier Walk, Chicago, IL
2005
Galleria d'Arte Benucci, Rome, Italy

SELECTED PUBLIC COLLECTIONS

Algoma Art Gallery, Ontario, Canada
Art Gallery of Hamilton, Hamilton, Ontario, Canada
Bank America, San Francisco, CA
Bridgewater State College, Bridgewater, MA
Centre Georges Pompidou, Beauborg, Paris
Continental Insurance Company, New York
Cornell Fine Arts Museum, Winter Park, FL
Denver Art Museum, Denver, CO
Des Moines Art Center, Des Moines, IA
Duke University, Durham, NC
Edmonton Art Gallery, Edmonton, Alberta, Canada
Everson Museum of Art, Syracuse, NY
Fogg Museum, Harvard University, Cambridge, MA
Simon Fraser University, Burnaby, British Columbia, Canada
Solomon R. Guggenheim Museum, New York
Hack Museum, Luduigshafen, Germany
Hamilton Art Gallery, Ontario, Canada
Hirshhorn Museum and Sculpture Garden, Washington, DC
Huntington Galleries, Huntington, WV
Kitchener-Waterloo Art Gallery, Kitchener, Ontario, Canada
Kunsthalle, Bielefeld, Germany
J. Patrick Lannan Foundation, Palm Beach, FL
Laumeier Sculpture Park, St. Louis, MO
Lehmbruck Museum, Duisburg, Germany
Massachusetts Institute of Technology Museum, Cambridge, MA
Musee d'Art Moderne et d'Art Contemporain, Nice, France
Museum of Fine Arts, Boston, MA
Museum of Fine Arts, Houston, TX
Museum of Modern Art, New York
Portland Art Museum, Portland, OR
Power Gallery of Contemporary Art, Sydney, Australia
J.B. Speed Art Museum, Louisville, KY
Museum Sprengee, Hanover, Germany
Macdonald Stewart Art Centre, Guelph, Ontario, Canada
Storm King Art Center, Mountainville, NY
Von der Heydt Museum, Wuppertge, Germany
Walker Art Center, Minneapolis, MN
Weathersoon Art Gallery, Greensboro, NC
Wellesley College, Wellesley, MA
Whitney Museum of American Art, NY

BIBLIOGRAPHY

Agee, William. *Michael Steiner: Bronze Sculpture 1979–1989*, Salander-O'Reilly Galleries, New York, 1990.
Agee, William. *Michael Steiner: Sculpture*, Salander-O'Reilly Galleries, New York, May 1990, exhibition catalogue.
"Album: Michael Steiner," *Arts Magazine*, September 1987, pp. 104–5.
"Art Museums Establish Deknatel Fund of Modern Art," Harvard University Gazette website (*www.hno.harvard.edu/gazette*), October 25, 2001.
"Art New England: A Resource for the Visual Arts," September 1985, with black and white reproduction, p. 21.
Arte Contemporaneo Norteamerican; Coleccion David Mirvish, American Embassy in Madrid, January 1984, p. 52, exhibition catalogue.

"Arthur K. Solomon, Faculty of Medicine: Memorial Minute," Harvard University Gazette website (*www.news.harvard.edu/gazette*), February 10, 2005.
Ashton, Dore. "New York Commentary," *Studio*, November 1967, p. 216.
Bannard, Walter Darby. *Michael Steiner: New Sculpture*, Meredith Long & Co., Houston, 1981, exhibition catalogue.
Bannard, Walter Darby. "Michael Steiner," *Cover*, #6, Winter 81/82, , pp. 42–27.
Benedict, Michael. "New York Letter," *Art International*, January 1967, p. 58.
Benedict, Michael. "Reviews and Previews," *ARTnews*, April 1968, p. 57.
Berman, Ann E. "Sculptors in Progress," *Town and Country*, September 1987, pp. 269–72.
Berrigan, Ted. "Reviews and Previews," *ARTnews*, November 1966, p. 68.
Blok, C. "Minimal Art at the Hague," *Art International*, May 1968, pp. 18–24.
Brenson, Michael. "Michael Steiner," *The New York Times*, review, November 11, 1983, p. C30.
Brenson, Michael. "Michael Steiner," *The New York Times*, January 3, 1986, p. C19.
"BSC receives gift of a Michael Steiner Sculpture," Bridgewater State College website (*www.bridgew.edu*), March 2005.
"Bronze at Washington Square," The Public Art Trust and the International Sculpture Center, Washington, DC, October 6, 1983–February 3, 1984, exhibition catalogue.
Cabanne, Pierre. "Cinq Grands Sculpteurs a la Galerie de France," *Le Matin de Paris*, March 26, 1980.
Carpenter, Ken. "New Works in Clay at the Edmonton Art Gallery," *Arts Magazine*, November–December 1978, pp. 40–43.
Cavaliere, Barbara. "Arts Reviews," *Arts Magazine*, June 1979, p.30.
Clark, Garth and Margie Hughto. *A Century of Ceramics in the United States, 1878–1978*, New York: E.P. Dutton in association with the Everson Museum of Art, Syracuse, New York, 1979.
"Contemporary Sculpture/André Emmerich," *The Wall Street Transcript*, vol. LXXVIII, no. 13, December 27, 1982, pp. 68/197, 68/236.
Crossley, Mimi. "Art: Sculpture by Michael Steiner," *Houston Post*, January 13, 1977.
Crossley, Mimi. Review, Meredith Long, *Houston Post*, October 24, 1981, p. 6F.
Dahlin, Robert. "Noted Sculptor Michael Steiner of Bridgewater: Master of Steel," *The Litchfield County Times*, May 25, 1990.
Danieli, Fidel A. "Los Angeles: New York Group at the Dwan Gallery," *Artforum*, April 1967, pp. 61–62.
Deschamps, Madeleine. "La Sculpture de Fer ou la Fuite du Centre," *Art Press* (Paris), March 1980, pp. 5–7.
Dienst, R.G. "Ausstellungen in New York," *Kunstwerk*, April 1968, pp. 23–24.
Elsen, Albert. *Casting: A Survey of Cast Metal Sculpture in the 80s*, Fuller Goldeen Gallery, San Francisco, CA, 1982, exhibition catalogue.
Fenton, Terry. "Michael Steiner," *Art International*, December 1970, pp. 34–36.
Fenton, Terry. "Michael Steiner," *Arts Magazine*, February 1974, pp. 72–74.
Fenton, Terry. "New Small Sculpture," *Update*, Edmonton Art Gallery, vol. 3, no. 6, November–December 1982, pp. 6–9.
Fermigier, Andre. "Cinq Sculpteurs a las Galerie de France," *Le Monde*, March 22, 1980, p. 1,30.
Fourcade, Dominique. "Michael Steiner," preface, André Emmerich Gallery, Zurich, October 1977, exhibition catalogue.

Fourcade, Dominique. "Michael Steiner," preface, André Emmerich Gallery, New York, January 1978.

Fourcade, Dominique. "Michael Steiner," *Art International*, November–December 1978, p. 41ff.

Fourcade, Dominique. *Michael Steiner: New Sculpture*, André Emmerich Gallery, New York, 1983, exhibition catalogue.

Ffrench–Frazier, Nina. Review, *Art International*, September–October 1980, pp. 98–99.

Frackman, Noel. *Arts Magazine*, April 1978, p. 31.

Fried, Michael. "Art and Objecthood," *Artforum*, Summer 1967, p.19.

Genocchio, Benjamin. "Evolving Through Sculpture," *The New York Times* (Westchester, Sunday, July 17, 2005; Connecticut, Sunday, July 24, 2005).

Gibson, Michael. "Around the Galleries," *International Herald Tribune*, February 23–24, 1980.

Gill, Susan. "Michael Steiner at André Emmerich," *ARTnews*, November 1987, p. 192.

Glueck, Grace. "Reviews and Previews," *Art in America*, January 1972, pp. 39–40.

Fourcade, Dominique. *Gonzalez/Smith/Caro/Scott/Steiner*, Galerie de France, Paris, 1980, exhibition catalogue.

Haden-Guest, Anthony. "Alternate States: City and Country Addresses of Phyllis and Michael Steiner," *Architectural Digest*, July 1986, pp. 40–47.

Hoesterey, Ingeborg. "New York," *Art International*, December 1975, p. 49.

Hoffman, Donald. "Sculptor's Twisting, Interwoven Planes Emerge with Flair," review of exhibition at Douglas Drake Gallery, *Kansas City Star*, September 1, 1985, p.6E.

Jablons, Pamela. "Collecting Within a Tradition," *Diversion*, August 1982, pp. 201–208.

Janis, Stefan. "Sculpture of Bridgewater's Steiner at N.Y. Gallery," *The Litchfield County Times*, November, 1993

Kim, Evangeline. "Michael Steiner in 1975," *Arts Magazine*, November 1975.

Kozloff, Max. "New York," *Artforum*, January 1967, p. 56.

L'Amerique aux Independants, 91e Exposition, Société des Artistes, Grand Palais, Paris, 1980, text by Lois de Menil, pp. 37, 62, 65.

Linville, Kasha. "In the Galleries: Steiner at Marlborough," *Arts Magazine*, Summer 1970, p. 60.

Lippard, Lucy. "New York Letter," *Art International*, February 1965, p. 37.

Lobell, John. "Developing Technologies for Sculptors," *Arts Magazine*, Summer 1971, pp. 27–29.

"Look at It, Climb on It, Drive on It," *St. Louis Post-Dispatch*, September 21, 1978.

Lorber, Richard. "Arts Reviews," *Arts Magazine*, January 1976, p. 12.

Margolies, John S. "In the Galleries," *Arts Magazine*, September–October 1967, p. 54.

Margolies, John S. "In the Galleries," *Arts Magazine*, April 1968, pp. 42–43.

Marshall, Neil W. "The New Sculpture of Michael Steiner," *Arts Magazine*, February 1978, pp. 134–5.

Mashek, Joseph. "New York: Michael Steiner," *Artforum*, September 1970, p. 80.

Mellow, James R. "New York Letter," *Art International*, Summer 1968, p. 108.

Mellow, James R. "Up Against the Wall or Floor," *The New York Times*, June 1970, pp. 19, 21.

"Michael Steiner," *The New York Times*, May 11, 1990.

Michael Steiner: Skulpturen, Amerika Haus, Berlin, August 30 October 13, 1979, essays by Dominique Fourcade and Kenworth Moffett.

Michael Steiner: Bronze Sculpture, André Emmerich Gallery, 1982, exhibition catalogue.

Michael Steiner, New Sculpture, André Emmerich Gallery, November 26, 1985–January 4, 1986, exhibition catalogue.

Moffett, Kenworth. "Michael Steiner," preface, Museum of Fine Arts, Boston, MA, March–April 1974, exhibition catalogue.

Moffett, Kenworth. *Moffett's Artletter*, vol.1, no. 5, July 1986, p.3.

Moffett, Kenworth. "Olitski: New Sculpture," *Art International*, March 1978.

Monte, James. "Emmerich Presents Steiner Exhibition," *Museum Magazine*, October 1981, p. 96S.

Moser, Charlotte. "Sleek Shapes, Sail Ships Spark Two Shows Here," *Houston Chronicle*, January 16, 1977, p. 11.

Museum of Art, Member Newsletter, "Steiner on Exhibit," Fort Lauderdale, Fl, Spring 1992.

New Prints, Dickenson Art Corporation, Great Neck, NY, 1981.

Pincus-Witten, Robert. "New York," *Artforum*, March 1967, p. 52.

Osborne, Harold. *The Oxford Companion to Twentieth Century Art*. New York: Oxford University Pres, 1981, p. 521.

Ratcliff, Carter. "New York Letter," *Art International*, September 1970, p. 91.

Ratcliff, Carter. "New York Letter," *Art International*, March 1972, p. 31.

Saunders, Wade. "Hot Metal," *Art in America*, Summer 1980, pp. 87–95.

Schjeldahl, Peter. "Steiner's Confidence," *Art in America*, October 1980, pp. 124–6.

Schuman, Jackie. "Best Bets on Gallery-Hopping in New York," *The Times-Union*, February 25, 1978.

"Sculpture, Both Material and Melodic," *The New York Observer*. November 1, 1999

"Sculpture in America/Connoisseur's Corner," *The Wall Street Transcript*, August 2, 1982, pp. 66/657, 66/709.

"Sculpture Newsletter," Storm King Art Center, Fall 1985, black and white reproduction, p. 2.

Secunda, Arthur. "In the Galleries: Michael Steiner at Goldowsky Gallery," *Arts Magazine*, March 1972, p. 61.

Selections from the William J. Hokin Collection, Museum of Contemporary Art, Chicago, 1985, plate 123, exhibition catalogue.

"Steiner Sculpture Exhibiiton at André Emmerich Gallery," *Antiques & The Arts Weekly*, September 11, 1987, p. 52.

Taplin, Robert, "Patterns of Mind," *Art in America*, April 2000, pp. 148–49 (review of Salander-O'Reilly Exhibition).

Tatransky, Valentin. "Michael Steiner," *Arts*, September 1982, p. 38 (review of André Emmerich Gallery exhibition).

Tatransky, Valentin. "Michael Steiner and Sculpture's History," *Arts Magazine*, November 1983, pp. 130–2.

Tatransky, Valentin. "Turning Down the Crew: On Michael Steiner," *Arts Magazine*, December 1981, pp. 158–60.

Tennant, Donna. "Sculptor Michael Steiner: A Rising Star," *Houston Chronicle*, November 16, 1980.

Virginia Dwan et Les Nouveaux Realistes, Los Angeles, Les Annees 60, Galeries Montaigne, Paris, 1990.

Weber, Nicholas Fox. "A Walk with Michael Steiner," exhibition catalogue. Grounds for Sculpture, NJ. 1998.

Wilkin, Karen. "At the Galleries," *Partisan Review*, August 1990.

Wilkin, Karen. "Michael Steiner," *Arts Magazine*, February 1984, p. 9.

Wilkin, Karen. *Michael Steiner: Recent Sculpture*, Gallery One, Toronto, 1981, exhibition catalogue.

Wilkin, Karen, "At the Galleries," *Partisan Review* (Winter 2002).

Wolmer, Denise. "In the Galleries: Michael Steiner at Marlborough Gallery," *Arts Magazine*, February 1974, pp. 72–74.

COVER: *Figure Turned Round*, 2005 (cat. no. 9)

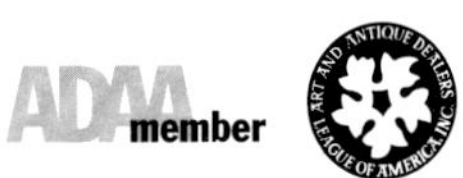

© 2006 Salander-O'Reilly Galleries, LLC
ISBN 1-58821-144-4
Photography: Maggie Nimkin
Design: Lawrence Sunden, Inc.
Printing: The Studley Press